THE GOD OF STONES AND SPIDERS

THE GOD
OF STONES
AND SPIDERS

Letters to a Church in Exile

Charles Colson

with Ellen Santilli Vaughn

CROSSWAY BOOKS • WHEATON, ILLINOIS
A DIVISION OF GOOD NEWS PUBLISHERS

The God of Stones and Spiders .

Copyright © 1990 by Charles Colson.

Published by Crossway Books, a division of
Good News Publishers, Wheaton, Illinois 60187.

Cover illustration: © 1990 SuperStock

Third printing, 1990

Printed in the United States of America

Library of Congress Catalog Card Number 90-81611

ISBN 0-89107-571-2

Contents

Introduction

Some of the Pharisees in the crowd said to Jesus, "Teacher, rebuke your disciples!" "I tell you," he replied, "if they keep quiet, the stones will cry out." (Luke 19:40)

It was twelve years ago that Alexander Solzhenitsyn stunned the distinguished audience assembled for Harvard's 327th commencement.

Sounding more like an Old Testament prophet than a Nobel Laureate, Solzhenitsyn charged intellectuals and the media with abandoning the West's Christian heritage and embracing instead a destructive humanism.

While the human spirit had been strengthened in the East through suffering, said Solzhenitsyn, the affluent and comfortable West had become spiritually exhausted. It had lost its courage and moral resolve.

Many dismissed the Russian writer's speech as an extremist's rantings. The suggestion of spiritual renewal in the East seemed unlikely at best; Communist tyrants held the church in an iron grip.

And in the West an unprecedented born-again movement antici-
pated a widespread return to traditional moral values.

But by 1990 Solzhenitsyn's startling words had proved
prophetic. A spiritual movement born in the open-air masses of
Krakow, the Lutheran churches of East Germany, and the sanctu-
aries of brave Romanian pastors had spilled onto the streets, top-
pling Communist tyrants. All the while the West, its born-again
enthusiasm spent, drifted far from its moral moorings.

A few months ago I traveled to Solzhenitsyn's native land.
There I saw firsthand the new spiritual openness in the East the
Russian writer had foretold.

I went to Russia to visit Soviet prisons, and in Moscow found
myself at a negotiating table across from Vadim Viktorovich
Bakatin, minister of internal affairs and fourth-ranking official in
the Communist government.

Mr. Bakatin is an impressive man with alert, penetrating eyes
and a hearty manner. He welcomed our delegation and opened the
meeting by explaining, with disarming candor, the crime problem in
the Soviet Union.

Crime shot up 38 percent in 1989, he said. The reasons were varied: economic, political, and ethnic unrest. But the Soviets were determined to improve their prison system and deal with their crime crisis.

I told him I had first traveled to the Soviet Union seventeen
years earlier as a negotiator for President Nixon. I said I had then
been caught in the Watergate mess, and had gone to jail. As this was
translated, he chuckled, and I felt a rapport building between us.

He had been candid; I returned the favor. I told him that crime
is *not* caused by economic or political or ethnic factors. It is caused
by sin—by the fundamental evil in the human heart.

In a system that rejects God, there can be no transcendent values or authority to which people are accountable—so one can only
reasonably expect unfettered human behavior. And that means
crime. "As your own writer Fyodor Dostoyevski put it in *The
Brothers Karamazov*," I said, "when there is no God, everything is
permitted. Crime becomes inevitable."

Then I described Prison Fellowship's ministry: how Christian volunteers visit prisons, sharing the news that Jesus can change an offender's heart and give him a new perspective for living. Bakatin listened intently. "That's what we need," he said.

Encouraged, I laid my hopes on the table. "This is what I would suggest," I said. "One, that religious services be allowed. Two, that community involvement be encouraged. Three, that after-care be developed, using community groups like Prison Fellowship. And four, that restitution and help for victims be made part of your criminal justice process."

Mr. Bakatin smiled broadly. "Mr. Colson," he said, "we will welcome Prison Fellowship and groups like you in our prisons. We need your kind of help." He paused, then with a twinkle in his eye concluded, "And God be with you."

Surprised and delighted as I was by this outcome, I'm not so naive as to suppose that Soviet officials have all suddenly been born again. But what is obvious is that they recognize the failure of the Communist system to provide any moral undergirding for their society.

Vladimir Shlapentokh, who conducted public opinion polls for *Pravda* and *Izvestia* before emigrating to the U.S., writes, "That the country is immersed in a moral crisis is now acknowledged by all." Soviet leaders are looking for help "in the form of the restoration of old religious norms . . . compassion, grace, forgiveness, charity, and other virtues previously presented as elements of bourgeois decadence." Leaders "[see] religion as a means of halting Soviet society's accelerating demoralization."

This is the great irony of our age. While formerly "godless Communists" are affirming the fact that society cannot survive without a vital religious influence, religion continues to be shoved out of the public square in what many used to call "Christian" America.

Privately-practiced religion is, I suppose, still acceptable here. But come out of your prayer closet and voice an opinion informed by religious values, and representatives from the liberal elite in our nation—educators, media moguls, attorneys, politicians, civil liberties groups—will have you for lunch.

They epitomize a force in our society preoccupied with scrubbing all religious influences from the public square. No opportunity is too high or too low to escape their attention: they've hired cranes to remove crosses atop steeples on college campuses, and donned scuba gear to dig up statues of Jesus from underwater sea parks.

They've been busy in other arenas as well.

In the arts and entertainment, public tax dollars have funded expressions offensive to at least one sector of the public, such as a crucifix submerged in urine. Television shows and film scripts consistently either ignore the existence of Christians altogether, or portray believers as hypocrites and oafs.

The schools have been particularly hard hit. High-school students in Decatur, Georgia, were informed that they could not wear their Fellowship of Christian Athletes T-shirts to school (though satanic T-shirts were OK). *The Last Temptation of Christ*, a tormented and blasphemous depiction of Jesus, was shown in an Albuquerque high school; one can only imagine the uproar if Christians attempted the showing of the Genesis Project's *Jesus* film, an accurate portrayal of the historical Christ, anywhere near school grounds.

School prayer is still banned; and kids in public-school sex education classes are taught about alternative homosexual lifestyles, condoms, and "safe sex" in a so-called "value-neutral" environment (though in fact values hostile to Christianity are perpetrated with impunity).

Perhaps most ludicrous of all, Christianity's role in history is being exorcised, like a pesky demon, from textbooks. Thanksgiving is now presented not as the day set aside so the Pilgrims, a deeply religious people, could thank God for His blessings. Rather, today students are informed that the feast day began when the Pilgrims "gave thanks to the Indians."

Tempting as it to believe, this is not happening because of some vast and sinister underground conspiracy to drive Christians and their influence from the planet. It is happening because Christians violate what has become the cardinal virtue of American life and culture: in an age that assumes the relativity of truth, we declare truth to be absolute, found in the person of Jesus Christ and the revelation of Scripture. What an anachronism! What an offense!

The paragons of tolerance who dominate the media, politics, education, and law purport to hold a tolerant and enlightened view toward any and all beliefs. Their modulated claims of "value-neutral" teaching, programming, or thinking, however, are a farce. Alleged neutrality is at war with values; tolerance proponents will tolerate just about anything, bending over backwards to avoid slurs against homosexuals, Buddhists, or crystal time-travelers.

But let a person motivated by orthodox Christian beliefs come to the fore and he will soon be dismissed. Even a hero like Vaclav Havel, darling of the Western media in the early part of 1990, was censored when he strayed too far from the generally-inspiring and into the Christian-specific. In its transcript of a Havel New Year's Day address, the *New York Times* deleted his references to "Jesus" and "the Christian spirit." Those who usually screech "Censorship!" at such moments were curiously silent.

Given the nineties' anti-Christian bias, there's a strong temptation to circle the wagons to defend ourselves against the slings and arrows of outrageous secularities . . . To cry foul and create a Christian anti-defamation league . . . To demand our rights and denounce our antagonists.

Surely this would make us all feel better. But such a strategy poses two dangers.

The first is that it wouldn't work, creating even more hostility.

The second, and greater, danger is that it might work. Suppose "anti-Christian bigotry" became as noxious a term as "anti-Semitism." Suppose city councils passed ordinances protecting us, like gays, against harassment. Suppose we succeeded in becoming a protected, persecuted minority.

Is this the Biblical vision for the people of God, for the holy nation? I think not. It would amount to a tragic surrender of our

Biblical commission to win men and women to Christ (which isn't accomplished by either hiding from them or poking them in the eye); to be salt and light; to let the blessings of God show forth in every area of life, as Cotton Mather once put it.

Where does today's hostility toward Christians leave us? Basically where the church has always been: at odds with the world. But that doesn't mean retreat; it means actively contending with the culture, debating and engaging our secular neighbors, helping them to see that they are dangerously adrift, that in fact the Judeo-Christian tradition provides the moral consensus upon which our rule of law rests, and that society desperately needs that foundation in order to survive. This must be part of our defense of truth in a pluralistic culture.

But we must defend the truth lovingly, winsomely, letting others see in all we do the excellence of Him who has called us from darkness into light.

This is no easy task. It is daunting and sometimes frightening. For though the forces that rise against us in these closing years of the century are civilized—after all, we don't have a Nero or a Ceaucescu seeking to stamp us out—their hostility to the Truth is no less real.

But it is crucial for us to remember that, regardless of how we feel, or how powerful seem the forces arrayed against us, the God we serve is sovereign. History is in His hands. And in times of greatest extremity He will raise up who He wills for His purposes. He will not lack for witnesses. This is a very freeing truth to remember.

Not surprisingly, that point was brought home to us most powerfully by the experience of a prisoner. She is a hero, both for her indomitable courage against overwhelming forces, and for the faith that fueled her courage.

Nien Cheng spent nearly seven years as a prisoner of the Red Guards during China's Cultural Revolution of the 1960s. It is her story that provides the lead essay and the title for this compilation. She is a woman who knows the truth of Luke 19:40—that a sovereign and mighty God will use the stones themselves, as Jesus said—or a tiny spider spinning an intricate web—to convey His grace and power in the face of opposition.

The following essays have been taken from regular columns of mine that were originally written for *Jubilee*, the newsletter of Prison Fellowship, or *Christianity Today*. It is the intent of these essays that the church in the West today—in so many ways captive to the forces of a hostile culture—would draw strength and renewed conviction for the battle. A good place to begin—particularly in light of Solzhenitsyn's prophetic message—is with the story of a prisoner in the East.

Charles W. Colson
Ellen Santilli Vaughn
May 1, 1990
P.O. Box 17500
Washington, DC 20041

PART I

Government and Public Policy

Chapter One

The God of Stones and Spiders

In Shanghai, they came for the university professors and businessmen first. Red Guards, some as young as fifteen, paraded them through the streets in dunce caps to hastily arranged tribunals. There, an act of "self-criticism" was demanded—confession to imaginary crimes against Mao Zedong. Most such criminals were sent to be "reeducated" in labor camps. Others were beaten or executed. The Great Proletarian Cultural Revolution had begun.

Mao's goal was to erase 6,000 years of Chinese law, manners, art, and history in one nationwide orgy of destruction and murder. With a society thus freed from tradition, he believed he could mold a new type of man—a Socialist man. Anyone who preserved the old ways, anyone with Western contacts, anyone with money, land, or education—all were "class enemies." Violent mobs of students, soldiers, and Party officials roamed the streets, attacking anyone with Western clothes or hairstyles, looting the homes of the wealthy. Death sentences were handed out like parking tickets.

Nien Cheng could see the circle of accusations tightening around her. A wealthy native of Shanghai, schooled in London and conversant in the art and music of East and West, she had worked for nine years at Shell Oil as a management adviser. Her neighbor, an engineer at a Swiss-owned aluminum company, was convicted as a "running dog of Swiss imperialism." His two young children joined in his denunciation, publicly severing their relationship with their faith. Nien Cheng was the Communists' next obvious target.

She prepared for her inevitable arrest like a woman planning a dinner party. Family heirlooms were packed away. Loyal servants were provided for. As raids on her home became more and more frequent, the teenaged Red Guards destroyed priceless porcelain and paintings. They viciously beat Nien Cheng and wrecked her home in search of nonexistent hoards of counterrevolutionary guns and gold.

Finally, on September 27, 1966, Nien Cheng was brought before a tribunal as an imperialist spy. As her accusers read a long list of false charges, others shouted angrily, "Confess! Confess!" Red Guards pulled at her clothes and spat on her jacket. "Dirty spy! We will kill you!"

"I have never done anything against the People's Government," Nien Cheng replied calmly.

She was taken to prison and locked into a small, damp cell. The single light bulb burned twenty-four hours a day. The bed and walls were caked with dirt.

Weeks passed. Nien Cheng dreamed of freedom and read the works of Mao, looking for passages to use against her accusers. And then, one day encouragement came from an unlikely source.

As Nien Cheng gazed out her tiny window, a pea-sized spider crawled through the rusty bars and climbed toward the ceiling. Suddenly the spider swung out on a silken thread, attached the strand to the base of the bar, and spun another, then another. It worked with purpose and confidence, weaving a web of intricate beauty.

"I had just watched an architectural feat by an extremely skilled artist," Nien Cheng writes of her tiny cell mate. "My mind was full of questions. Who had taught the spider to make a web? Could it have really acquired the skill through evolution, or did God create the spider and endow it with the ability to make a web so that it could catch food and perpetuate its species? . . . I knew I had just witnessed something that was extraordinarily beautiful and uplifting. Whether God had made the spider or not, I thanked Him for what I had just seen. It helped me to see that God was in control. Mao Zedong and his revolutionaries seemed much less menacing. I felt a renewal of hope and confidence."

That hope sustained Nien Cheng through six and a half years in prison; she was released without ever making the false confession her jailers demanded. Like Armando Valladares and Alexander Solzhenitsyn, Nien Cheng provides one of those extraordinary testimonies to the human spirit that come from prisons around the world. All the barbarism of the Cultural Revolution was set against the will of this delicate but determined woman. And she would not be changed.

But this is not just a story about the human spirit; it is a story about God and His sovereign power.

We in the West so carefully plan our evangelistic crusades and fund our missionary campaigns; soon we begin to believe that God's work depends on us. After all, without our efforts where would His Kingdom be? But this is a heretical illusion. A God limited to human crusades and campaigns is a God too small.

When Jesus was descending the Mount of Olives, His disciples broke into shouts and songs praising Him. The Pharisees, in typical ill-humor, told Jesus to shut them up. He replied, "I tell you, if these become silent, the stones will cry out!"

January 1988

Chapter Two

Images of the Eighties: Hope for the Nineties?

Historians, as the eminent Daniel Boorstin notes, like to "bundle" history in decades and centuries "as if God had designed the world on the decimal system." Perhaps that is why we always seem so optimistic about each new decade: It's a fresh chapter of history.

On the surface there is surely reason for optimism about this one: The economy is strong; remarkably, communism is crumbling; peace exists in most of the world.

But beneath the surface is a certain uneasiness. It's hard to muster enthusiasm for the nineties when the eighties have left us, to borrow a phrase from Alexander Solzhenitsyn's prophetic 1978 Harvard address, "morally exhausted."

Surely the images of the eighties evoke a sense of exhaustion:
- Ivan Boesky and ilk using insider information to swindle billions from the public.
- Public servants cynically skimming millions from HUD programs for the poor.
- Military officers trading honor for money or sex.
- S&Ls being looted for a staggering $150 billion.
- Scores of politicians being caught in scandals of greed or sex.

- Religious hucksters carving out personal fiefdoms.
- And a government that, in a decade of unmatched prosperity, tripled the national debt from one trillion to three trillion dollars, a self-indulgent binge at the expense of future generations.

A common thread runs through these images: the notion that life somehow gives us the *right* to have every whim and desire satisfied.

Just look at the reactions of those caught in the scandals. Seldom was heard a repentant word. "We were just doing what comes naturally" seemed to be the rationale. Boesky was merely an aggressive free-enterpriser. The S&L operators bought control and thus the *right* to do their own deals. Jim Bakker said he "earned" multimillion-dollar bonuses. Politicians defended their excesses as the perks of their office.

This is nothing less than a looter's ethic—each person grabbing whatever he can and calling it his right. But for me, nothing typifies the decade's moral rootlessness more than the remarkable turnabout in the abortion debate.

I first became involved in politics in the 1956 presidential campaign and have seen over the years how volatile political issues can be. But I've never witnessed anything like the recent flip-flop in the wake of the Supreme Court's *Webster* decision allowing states to limit abortions.

Before *Webster* a poll found that 57 percent believed abortion to be murder. The Republican platform was unequivocally pro-life, and a majority of politicians across the country opposed abortion. The *Webster* decision should have meant that at least half the state legislatures would vote to curb abortions.

But instead the political ground suddenly shifted as pro-choice support surged. Pro-life Republican gubernatorial candidates in New Jersey and Virginia backpedaled, but in vain; they were beaten on that issue. A conservative legislature in Florida rejected any abortion restrictions, as did several others. Across the country conservative politicians read the polls and, with a few courageous exceptions, fled in droves from their once rock-solid pro-life platforms. More than forty-five House members altered their positions.

What caused such a sudden and dramatic shift?

Before *Webster* the abortion issue was academic. Thanks to *Roe v. Wade*, the right to abortion was guaranteed under the banner of what the Court called an individual's right to privacy. No reason to get excited; one could decry the evil of abortion, knowing full well that no one's *right* could be taken away.

But after *Webster*, the issue was no longer academic. And pro-choice politicians and groups shrewdly reframed the debate in terms that frightened constituents. I saw one negative political commercial charging that a pro-life candidate "wants to take away your *right*." The media obliged them. On one newscast pro-choice demonstrators were four times labeled "abortion *rights* demonstrators"; the anchorman talked of "*rights* that are now in danger in this campaign." The word "pro-choice" has been almost completely replaced by "abortion rights," a subtle but powerful change.

An abstract moral principle has proved no match for the individual's sacred *right*. So in a matter of weeks public opinion dramatically swung about—with politicians falling all over themselves to stay on the right side.

Solzhenitsyn has compared America's obsession with rights to a person trying to breathe with only one lung. "There is another lung," says Solzhenitsyn, "and it is called duty."

People with one lung have high mortality rates. And so it is for societies in which individuals abandon their sense of duty, refusing to deny themselves for the common good and for the sake of others, including the defenseless and the unborn.

If moral exhaustion and rootlessness define the eighties, what of the nineties? Is there hope?

Yes, but only as those of us who are called to love our neighbor as ourselves set the example—and by word and deed convince a self-indulgent society that rights cannot long exist without a corresponding sense of duty.

January 1990

Chapter Three

Are We Ready for a Long Battle?

It was a chilly afternoon, January 22, 1988—fifteen years since the day in 1973 when the Supreme Court legalized abortion-on-demand. Some 50,000 protesters massed behind the White House to mark the gruesome anniversary; senators, representatives, and religious leaders passionately called for renewed pro-life commitment, a constitutional amendment to ban abortion, and an end to federal funding.

But hardly a word was said about reversing *Roe v. Wade* in the Supreme Court.

It seemed a curious omission. For seven years the expectation had been that President Reagan would appoint enough justices to overturn the landmark case. Yet now, when victory might likely be in sight with the appointment of Anthony Kennedy, a devout Catholic, many in the pro-life movement had grown skeptical about prospects for the long-awaited judicial turnaround. Why?

I believe the answer lies in understanding the Senate rejection of Kennedy's ill-fated forerunner, Judge Robert Bork. Ironically, Bork's very nomination may have actually solidified *Roe v. Wade* in the law.

Despite the various smoke screens and false trails created by the anti-Bork forces, the nomination battle centered on one issue: whether or not the Constitution provides a right to privacy.

This question is central to *Roe v. Wade*. Anyone who would seek to overturn the decision would be forced to question whether the right to privacy applies to having an abortion, or whether such a right exists at all.

Bork might have sidestepped this issue during his Senate inquisition. But instead he refused to disavow his views on the right to privacy; he held firm on earlier uncompromising statements, such as his description of *Roe v. Wade* as "an unconstitutional decision, a serious and wholly unjustified usurpation of state legislative authority."

The Senate responded with equal ardor, rejecting Judge Bork by a vote of 58-42. That rejection came not because of insufficient qualifications or lack of judicial temperament. Bork was turned down because of his opposition to the constitutional right to privacy—in other words, for threatening *Roe v. Wade*.

This fact was clear when Judge Kennedy was later confirmed. During his hearings, one senator read a long list of quotes from both Kennedy and Bork. On nearly every point of judicial philosophy and criminal justice theory their positions were identical. The single major exception? The right to privacy.

The signal the Senate has sent will not be lost on the Court. For judges don't decide cases in a vacuum. They carefully weigh legislative history and political judgments made by elected bodies and rely heavily on *stare decisis*, the precedent of decisions made in the past. Every Court ruling since 1973 to 1988 has affirmed *Roe v. Wade*; now the Senate seems to have put its legislative imprimatur on the right to abortion.

Thus, though I hope I'm wrong, my hunch is that neither Judge Kennedy nor even perhaps the other Reagan appointees to the Court will be inclined to oppose this established will of the Congress and fifteen years of judicial precedent.

Is this too grim an outlook?

Consider what may be the most comparable historical precedent. In 1856, the Supreme Court held that slaves were property; slaveholders were free to keep them in any federal territory. The *Dred Scott* decision was surely as unconscionable a ruling as *Roe v. Wade*, but it became the law of the land.

As such, it was hotly contested. Anti-slavery lawyers led a vigorous attack. Legislatures in Ohio, Vermont, and Maine passed resolutions assailing it. Church groups and the press—an unusual coalition—denounced it.

But in spite of this public outrage, the Supreme Court never reversed the *Dred Scott* decision. It eventually took the Thirteenth Amendment to the Constitution to bring an end to slavery.

Today we face a similar situation. I fear that the Court will be as unwilling to reverse *Roe v. Wade* as it was *Dred Scott*. And that means that nothing short of a constitutional amendment will bring an end to a practice as morally offensive as slavery.

The question that Christians must ask is whether or not we have the courage and perseverance to sustain a protracted national campaign for such an amendment. Today we lack the necessary majority in both Congress and the state legislatures, and, according to pollsters, public opinion is evenly divided. Thus our task will be to pierce the hardened conscience of our nation and build a new political consensus in three-quarters of the states. A seemingly insurmountable challenge.

But another historical example offers us hope. When the Christian politician William Wilberforce first denounced England's slave trade, he stood against deeply entrenched political and economic interests. He stood as well against courts that had held that slaves were nothing more than property.

Despite the overwhelming opposition, Wilberforce and a small band of like-minded Christians persisted. They prayed for three hours a day, circulated anti-slavery literature, mobilized churches and citizens' groups. And in the end they triumphed with a glorious victory that stamped out the slave trade.

But what was not so glorious was the fact that their campaign took twenty years. They were defeated time after time in the House of Commons. They were lampooned in political cartoons, snubbed by governmental leaders, and exhausted by their arduous efforts. But they refused to give up their cause.

If I am correct that *Roe v. Wade* cannot be upset in the Court, then it must be upset in the Constitution. To thus end the killing of the unborn, we must exercise the same holy tenacity demonstrated by those who fought slavery.

The immensity of the task ahead is sobering. We have no alternative but to persevere.

March 1988

Chapter Four

Abortion Clinic Obsolescence

This is a time of tragic irony for the right-to-life movement—for at the same time pro-life activists are courageously escalating their fight for life, events and technology are conspiring to render such efforts moot.

Let me explain.

Last fall [1988] Operation Rescue hit the streets and television screens of America. During the last weekend in October 1988, 2,212 pro-life supporters were arrested for blocking access to abortion clinics in thirty-two cities, bringing to 7,000 the number of pro-life arrests since the Democratic Convention the previous July.

Why this sudden intensification of pro-life commitment—this new willingness to sacrifice?

Some of the urgency may well come from desperation. After all the promises of the Reagan years, pro-life forces have few victories to show for all their efforts. Few expect that George Bush will manage to get much of the social agenda that Ronald Reagan could not. Civil disobedience, for some, may vent years of frustration.

But from what I have seen of Operation Rescue, this is not the whole story. Their anti-abortion sit-ins are not publicity stunts.

They are attempts to save lives based on clear-cut beliefs. Christy Anne Collins, a pro-life leader in the Washington area, has been jailed several times. As she describes her motivation, "The fact of the matter is, God said it's a crime to shed innocent blood. I think we have to stop the killing. If we believe that abortion is murder, and I do, then I think we have to act like it is murder and try to stop it."

Some Christian leaders have argued that Operation Rescue shows disrespect for the law. But to say that a law may never be violated under any circumstances is a form of extremism more disturbing than anything done by pro-life activists. Certainly one could justly break a no-trespassing law to save a child drowning in a lake; Operation Rescue, I believe, is the moral equivalent. Placing the value of a just law against trespassing above the attempted rescue of innocent lives is an inversion of Christian priorities.

It is a sad commentary that we live in a nation that puts such rescuers in jail. They are the most unlikely of prisoners. They are often intensely religious, both Protestant and Catholic. They have a deep respect for the law, though they value life more. They are nonviolent, but they are not easily intimidated.

These are, in short, the best of citizens—people who would be valued by any government under normal circumstances. But they populate our jails. It is a telling question: what kind of society would force its best citizens to violate the law as a matter of conscience?

But just as these principled protesters were indicting a calloused American conscience, events were taking place an ocean away that may soon render their protests impotent altogether.

On October 28, 1988, a day that saw a number of Operation Rescue arrests, the French government ordered a pharmaceutical company to resume distribution of RU 486—the abortion pill. Under pressure from pro-life groups, the company had earlier withdrawn it; but France's Socialist government ordered the drug back on the market, asserting that it was "the moral property of women."

The pill, in effect, causes an early miscarriage. It means that a home abortion could eventually be as close as two tablets and a glass of water. It means fast, effective relief—like Alka Seltzer or Tylenol.

Certainly there are things that can and should be done to restrict the availability of RU 486 in the U.S. Experiments with the drug are already being conducted here, though it will be several years before it could be approved by the Food and Drug Administration. Pro-life groups must make it clear to American politicians, health officials, and businessmen that this drug must not be legalized.

But the drug is already in use in China and Thailand. Populous Third World countries have made it clear they will be customers. Because it replaces surgery, the drug could easily be used on women who have little or no access to medical care.

And if RU 486 is used this widely, it would be impossible to prevent the creation of a black market. American demand would be high. Columnist Ellen Goodman comments, "Even if the opposition manages a legal ban, the abortion pill will become available. These pills are called in the trade 'bathtub' drugs; they are easy to make. . . . Anyone who believes that we could control their importation hasn't checked the cocaine business recently."

Faye Wattleton, president of Planned Parenthood, gloats that the "right-to-life movement has seen its last gasp. If these drugs get to the market, the fight is finally all over."

What response is left to us?

Of course we must fight for legal restrictions. But the effect of any law is bound to be limited, given the size of demand and the extent of legal distribution. And of course we must continue to protest. But abortion clinics in the future may well be necessary only for the few. How do you intervene to save a life when an abortion is as near as the medicine cabinet?

What RU 486 will eventually mean, I fear, is a dramatic shift in the rules of the abortion battle. It will mean that our fight against abortion will no longer focus on the clinic, the dumpster, the Supreme Court steps. It will be relational and educational:

Christians persuasively pressing the point among their peers that a life conceived is precious to God and must not be poisoned by a pill. The struggle will no longer be focused on legislatures and suction machines, but on people and the individual values they hold, the values that create their choices. What it means is changing the hearts and minds of a self-centered, callous generation.

That is a challenge perhaps even more daunting than the threat of a prison cell.

February 1989

Chapter Five

Equal Justice and the Abortion Clinic Bombers

In his fifth-century classic *The City of God*, Augustine argued that justice and concord are essential for the survival of society. "In the absence of justice," he wrote, "what is sovereignty but organized brigandage?"

Fifteen hundred years later, our American system of justice is, I believe, the best the world has to offer. But there are times when Lady Justice drops her blindfold—and the resulting selective justice brings Augustine's words to mind.

Consider the case of Matthew Goldsby and James Simmons, arrested for a Florida abortion clinic bombing. They were pilloried in the press, swiftly tried, convicted, and sentenced to ten years in prison —ironic, I thought, considering the celebrity status conferred at about the same time on Bernhard Goetz, the instant hero who has yet to be tried [1986] for shooting four young thugs on a New York subway.

I had almost recovered from my sense of outrage when I learned that Goldsby and Simmons had applied for parole—and were turned down. Though federal prisoners are eligible after one-third of their sentence, they were told not to reapply until 1990. And there's no assurance they'll get out then.

31

One might conclude that our system of justice excuses blowing away would-be muggers, but throws the book at those who blow up buildings. We don't mess around with wild-eyed zealots who use explosives to voice their consciences.

But it's not that simple. Evidently the system is choosy about what kind of zealots it prosecutes. For while the parole commission was leaving Goldsby and Simmons behind bars, the New York Bar Association was considering the admission of one Bernadine Dohrn.

Ms. Dohrn was, in the sixties, a leader of the Weathermen, an underground movement committed to the violent overthrow of the United States government. Dohrn and her friends boasted of more than two dozen bombings; later one of their explosives factories blew up, killing three people. Bombs also exploded at the U.S. Capitol and the Pentagon.

Their goal, they said, was to "kill all the rich people, break up their cars and apartments, bring the revolution home, kill your parents, that's where it's really at."

Charged with participating in bombing conspiracies, Bernadine Dohrn became a fugitive for ten years. She resurfaced in 1980, saying she still believed "in the necessity of underground work." Hardly the words of a repentant sinner.

After refusing to cooperate with the grand jury, Dohrn spent seven months in jail. On her release she still refused to cooperate. Husband Bill Ayers, another key underground figure, cheerfully described her case to *Rolling Stone*: "guilty as hell, free as a bird . . . America is a great country." Yes, I guess so, for people who blow up government buildings.

But now that she is seeking to practice law, Bernadine Dohrn has been repackaged by the likes of her father-in-law, former chairman of Commonwealth Edison and board member of the *Chicago Tribune*, and her attorney, Don Rubin, of a prominent Chicago law firm. Rubin says Dohrn is now "so conservative, she's dull."

Former federal judge Harold Tyler, Jr. has also supported the newly dull Dohrn, saying, "We're hopeful that they [the bar association] will feel she has been what I would call rehabilitated. . . . She acts like a perfectly typical lawyer in a big firm." (I'm not sure how "typical" lawyers in big firms might feel about this.)

Though Dohrn lost her first appeal for admission, her high-priced practitioners continue the fight. Meanwhile she's comfortably ensconced in her posh Manhattan apartment with her husband and three children.

And abortion clinic bombers Goldsby and Simmons—those wild-eyed religious zealots—sit in clammy prison cells.

What are we to make of all this?

First, the obvious conclusion. If you're contemplating blowing up any buildings, your best bet is the Capitol of the United States—and do it in the name of political fanaticism. Then go into hiding and return to society a decade later, unrepentant, continuing your vow to destroy the rich and beat the pigs. It helps, of course, to have powerful financial and political connections.

But if you happen to be a committed Christian, horrified that unborn children are being massacred in abortion clinics, and you get carried away by religious zealotry and break the law, be prepared for the scorn of the press and five to ten years in prison.

Ironically, in this country, whose motto is "one nation under God," political fanatics seem to fare better than religious zealots. Lady Justice, it seems, has lost not only her blindfold, but her balance as well.

I think Augustine had a point. In the Judeo-Christian view, rule is by law and not man. Without such impartial justice, government becomes no more than organized brigandage. These are strong words, but can anything less be said while bombers of some buildings lounge free in Manhattan apartments, and bombers of other buildings sit in prison awaiting distant parole dates?

April 1986

Chapter Six

The Fear of Doing Nothing

Joan Andrews does not look like a criminal. Slight, soft-spoken, a devout Roman Catholic, easily moved to tears—this is not the typical profile of an inmate at a maximum-security prison. But Joan Andrews is nonetheless one year into a five-year sentence at Broward Correctional Institute, a Florida women's prison [written in 1987].

I have visited Broward. Many of its prisoners are drug offenders or violent criminals. Homosexuality is rampant. It is a stark, maximum-security joint.

This is the last place you would expect to find Joan Andrews, known to her friends as "Saint Joan." But this is the same woman whom a judge pronounced an "unrepentant" felon.

Her crime? On March 26, 1986, she entered a Florida abortion clinic for a pro-life sit-in and attempted to unplug a suction machine used to perform abortions. She was charged and convicted of criminal mischief, burglary, and resisting arrest without violence.

The prosecution asked for a one-year sentence. The judge gave her five.

Miss Andrews announced to the court, "The only way I can

protest for unborn children now is by noncooperation in jail." She then dropped to the courtroom floor and refused to cooperate with prison officials at any stage of her processing. Labeled a troublemaker, she was transferred to Broward where, as of this writing, she remains in a solitary-confinement cell.

On one level, surely, this is an outrage. The day Andrews was sentenced, two men convicted as accessories to murder stood before the same judge. He sent them to prison for four years. Five years in a maximum-security prison for Joan Andrews's "crimes," which stem from moral conviction rather than moral deficiency, is disproportionately harsh.

But Joan Andrews's case raises questions that go beyond the justice of her sentence. Her case highlights some of the central tensions intrinsic to the issues of civil disobedience.

As citizens of both the Kingdom of God and the kingdoms of man, Christians owe loyalties to each. The governing authorities are to be obeyed—they are established by God to preserve order and seek justice. Yet our unconditional obedience belongs to God alone.

When our dual allegiances are at odds, there can be no question which takes precedence. Christians must recognize a transcendent order that guides their actions even when it stands in opposition to human law.

The Apostles Peter and John offer the classic example. When commanded by Jewish authorities not to teach in the name of Jesus, they refused. "We cannot stop talking about what we have seen and heard," they said. "Judge for yourselves whether it is right in God's sight to obey you rather than God." But significantly, they also acknowledged the right of civil authorities to punish them if their actions broke man's law.

Thus a law prohibiting the propagation of the gospel must be disobeyed, with believers prepared to pay the consequences.

Unfortunately, today's cases are often more ambiguous. Many involve the emotional issue of abortion. Some pro-life activists seek to use civil disobedience, particularly sit-ins, as a manner of expressing their protest. Trespassing is thus a means of making a political and moral statement while attracting public attention to injustice.

However, in an open society there are other legal means available to express political opposition. The options for the protester are many: picket, vote, organize, advertise, write your Congressman, or try to take his job. But we are not to abandon our belief in the rule of law, the foundation for public order, simply to make statements that could be made legally in other forums. Though there are many views among Christians regarding a Biblical perspective on civil disobedience, I have come to believe that, generally speaking, it is not justified to break a just law in order to protest an unjust law.

But this is not the end of the matter. Some civil disobedience by pro-life groups is undertaken for a different reason. Rather than a form of protest—or perhaps in addition—it is intended to save lives at risk.

There are values higher than the law. One of them, certainly, is the value of life, the principal value law is intended to protect. In instances where it is threatened, the law must give way. A lake marked "No Trespassing" is legally off-limits under normal circumstances. But to save a drowning child, the law could justifiably be broken.

A "rescue mission" at an abortion clinic can be analogous. The requirement to obey a just law (trespassing) is superseded by the possibility of saving a life. Those who are stirred to such rescue action, however, must affirm their belief in the values of law by being prepared to accept the consequences of breaking it.

Joan Andrews is such a person. I have not been able to talk with her regarding her views on the fine points of Biblical justifications for civil disobedience. Clearly some of her actions, such as refusing to submit to prison authorities, conflict with the Biblical standard of Romans 13.

But one thing is clear. Joan Andrews's conscience would not allow her to pass by on the other side of the street while unborn babies were being murdered. What she did came naturally. When Joan was twelve, her cousin was carried away by a river current while swimming. Joan, a poor swimmer, was paralyzed with fear.

"I thought if I tried to save her, we would both drown," she says today. "But then a greater fear grabbed me, the fear of doing nothing." Joan jumped into the churning water and saved her cousin.

Today this courageous young woman, still motivated by the fear of doing nothing in the face of death, is paying the price for her convictions: five years in prison.

So she sits hunched in a small, solitary-confinement cell, often in prayer—a silent symbol indicting a nation sanctioning the murder of millions of the defenseless.

May 1987

Chapter Seven

The Little Platoons and the Big War

Two recent developments [1986] in the decades-long struggle against pornography give us an instructive lesson in what really creates change in American society. Just last month, after a year's descent into the murky world of smut, the Attorney General's Commission on Pornography surfaced. Its task, given by President Reagan, had been to study pornography and to "tell America what to do about it."

A tall order. The commission's charter took it into an arena where different perspectives passionately clash: the economic interests of the massive pornography industry; the concerns of civil libertarians, who see specters of censorship lurking in every paragraph; and the concerns of Christians, who see pornography as an odious symptom of widespread moral rot.

Pornography's adversaries have pinned great hopes on the panel's recommendations. After all, working through the leverage of big government seems the most effective way to destroy such a widespread social cancer.

As one of the nation's least-regulated industries (earning six billion dollars last year), pornography recognizes few standards except the increasingly perverse tastes of its clientele. Michigan police statistics show that pornography was involved in 40 percent of its sexual assault cases. The FBI Academy issued a report tracing pornography's role in fantasies prior to sexual murder.

The Meese commission, which included Focus on the Family's Dr. James Dobson, found similar evidence. Dobson said the job, which included twelve-hour days of wading through material such as "Pregnant Lesbians" and "Tri-Sexual Lust," was one of the most unpleasant experiences of his life. "I will never forget a particular set of photographs . . ." he says. "It focused on a cute nine-year-old boy who had fallen into the hands of a molester. In the first picture, the blond lad was fully clothed and smiling at the camera. But in the second, he was nude, dead, and had a butcher knife protruding from his chest. I . . . thought I had seen it all. But my knees buckled, and tears came to my eyes. . . ."

Christians should be grateful to James Dobson for taking on such a tough task. Because of his leadership, the report may now set the tone for national policies for years to come. The panel's report strongly supports the connection between some pornography and violent crimes. It also recommends tougher prosecution practices, stronger federal laws, and the vigorous enforcement of existing obscenity laws.

But just because the report is finished doesn't mean the problem is solved. Even if these laudable proposals make it through the legislative process—and that will be tough going—extended court challenges can be expected. Balancing free speech against the right of public freedom from smut is a delicate business. Purveyors of pornography have prevailed in many court decisions in the past; and as Barry Lynn of the American Civil Liberties Union has boasted, "There are enough constitutional questions here to litigate for the next 20 years."

So, while we must keep fighting through litigation and legislation, we must also be realistic: nothing in the record of recent years offers much hope that pornography's surging tides can be easily stemmed in the courts or in the halls of Congress.

But even as the Commission was finishing its report, the pornography industry did suffer its first major blow in years—in a way that caught just about everyone by surprise.

When Jack Eckerd, founder of the Eckerd Drug chain, became a Christian in 1983, he gained a new perspective on the *Playboy* and *Penthouse* magazines sold in his stores. He called his company's president and told him he wanted the magazines out. The executive protested. Jack Eckerd persisted. Eventually all 1,700 Eckerd drugstores dropped their copies of *Playboy* and *Penthouse*.

Eckerd wrote to the directors of other retail stores, encouraging them to stop stocking the magazines. When his letters went unanswered, he wrote again.

Meanwhile, thousands of Christians, organized under the National Coalition Against Pornography, were taking the stand as well—through widespread picketing and a boycott of stores selling "adult magazines."

The pressure began to pay off. Like dominoes, stores began to remove *Playboy* and *Penthouse*. One by one Revco, Peoples, Rite-Aid, Dart Drug, Gray Drug, and High's Dairy Stores all pulled pornography from their shelves.

And finally, last April [1986], the last major holdout gave in as well: 7-Eleven removed pornography from its 4,500 stores and recommended that its 3,600 franchises do the same.

Thus, without one debate before Congress or one case won in the courts, nearly 12,000 retail stores have cleaned pornography from their shelves!

Playboy's lawyers, shocked at the blow, are arguing that a letter written from the Meese commission put coercive pressure on the stores. Maybe it did have an impact. But the real impetus came not from the government, but from the inexorable pressure of thousands of Christians and the courageous action of one man who was converted and immediately put his faith into practice right in his own line of business.

This victory against a formidable foe has given many Christians a renewed vision—moral change is possible after all!

The nineteenth-century English political writer Edmund Burke would have applauded such strategy. He wrote about the value of "little platoons"—private, voluntary groups of people that shape the conscience of a country and accomplish far more than the machinations of big government.

In today's culture, obsessed with solutions that come from the top down, this is a radical notion. But as the anti-pornography campaign makes clear, we don't need to place all our hopes in government. When we accept personal responsibility to act as salt and light right where we are, the results can be spectacular. Our "little platoons," like Gideon's tiny band, can put the greatest armies to flight.

August 1986

Chapter Eight

Ted Bundy's Legacy

When mass murderer Ted Bundy went to the electric chair last January [1989], millions of outraged Americans, regardless of their stand on the death penalty, felt an odd sense of relief. At last the long Bundy nightmare was over.

But Bundy did contribute something to us before he died. In his celebrated interview with Dr. James Dobson, Bundy spoke candidly of his long involvement with pornography. Starting as a child, he graduated to more and more extreme forms of smut. His murders fused his fascinations with twisted sex and violent death.

Bundy was an aberration. But he was also a warning. Though many secular observers are unwilling to link pornography with violent crime, growing evidence suggests a direct link between pornography and increased levels of violence. An FBI Academy report convincingly traced pornography's role in fantasies prior to sex-related murders, and a study from the Michigan State Police linked pornography to 40 percent of its assault cases.

All of this makes a little-known case in the U.S. District of Iowa shocking. Only a few months before Bundy's execution,

Federal Judge Harold Vietor prevented prison officials from keeping pornography out of Iowa's prisons.

The case began when several Iowa inmates objected to a prison policy allowing officials to screen prisoners' mail. Material that officials deemed threatening to security or rehabilitation—publications depicting sexually explicit, violent, or deviant behavior—was routinely censored. A reasonable enough policy.

Not to Judge Vietor. The inmates brought their case, *Dawson v. Scurr*, on First-Amendment grounds—and the judge ruled in their favor, stating that "prisoners should be entitled to the same magazines available to other Iowans."

As a result, Iowa prisons were forced to set up controlled areas where prisoners could read the previously screened materials. The image of inmates perusing porn in these "reading rooms" should raise the hackles of Iowa taxpayers.

This outrageous decision caused me to examine policies in other jurisdictions. Most prisons in the U.S., including federal institutions, are permitted to block materials legally classified as obscene—such things as bestiality, sadomasochism, and child pornography. But Iowa had been almost alone in blocking material deemed merely sexually explicit. Nearly every other state and the federal system allows prisoners to receive this "soft-core" porn through the mail.

Meanwhile, the American Civil Liberties Union, claiming that prison officials' screening discretion was too broad and thus quashed inmates' rights, navigated a case to the U.S. Supreme Court. *Thornburgh v. Abbott* challenged federal prison policies allowing officials to censor pornographic publications according to their own standards of what was dangerous to prison order and security.

Thankfully, the Court ruled to affirm the government's general discretion in screening materials. But it sent forty-six publications that had been blocked on occasion back to the lower court for review. If the lower court rules that such publications can freely reach inmates' cells, it will further swell the tide of pornography streaming into U.S. prisons.

So on the one hand we have a horrifying firsthand account of how pornography poisoned a horrendous mass murderer; on the other, we have apparently serious-minded people who want to permit that same kind of pollutive material into our overcrowded prisons—places already seething with sexual frustration and aggression.

Common sense would compel us not to allow convicted arsonists the right to receive blowtorches in the mail. Nor should violent offenders receive pornography—any kind of pornography—as a prison courtesy.

Lest anyone misunderstand, I am sympathetic with the need to protect inmates' rights. After all, I spent time in a federal prison. But when I did so, I realized that I surrendered certain freedoms. My mail was censored and my phone calls tapped. I understood that inherent in confinement was the loss of rights that could threaten institutional security.

It seems that the ACLU and Judge Vietor see prisons as places where inmates should enjoy the same rights as free citizens—whether or not they threaten security or jeopardize inmates' rehabilitation.

This is dangerous nonsense. Pornography not only degrades humanity, it splinters the picture of wholeness we hold forth to offenders. How can we encourage prisoners to learn to build relationships and live in community while allowing explicit and often violent pornography in our "correctional" institutions, spreading images of the most perverse and broken of worlds?

In yet another irony regarding inmate rights, last year the U.S. Supreme Court refused to order prison officials to adjust work assignments so inmates could attend worship services. Although no one disputed the sincerity of the prisoners' religious convictions (who were, it is only fair to point out, represented by the ACLU), the Court ruled that "institutional order and security" outweighed the inmates' religious rights.

In the light of these decisions, it would seem to say that an inmate's right to pornography has greater constitutional protection than his right to worship.

Disturbing developments. But in an age in which good and evil are often confused, perhaps we shouldn't be surprised.

July 1989

Chapter Nine

It's Not Over, Debbie

The scene is a darkened hospital ward. An intern stands over Debbie, a young woman with terminal cancer. Her breathing is labored as she struggles for oxygen. She weighs eighty pounds. She is in horrible pain.

The doctor has never seen Debbie before, but a glance at her chart confirms she is not responding to treatment. He leans down to hear her whisper, "Let's get this over with."

Most doctors would have hurried to give relief against the pain, or tried to offer some solace to the anguished relative standing near the bed. But this intern measured out 20 milligrams of morphine into a syringe—enough, he wrote later, "to do the job"—and injected it. Four minutes later Debbie was dead. The doctor's only comment: "It's over, Debbie."

Stories like this are shocking, but should not surprise us. While no one likes to admit it, active euthanasia is not uncommon. It has been closeted in hospital ethics committees, or cloaked in euphemisms spoken to grieving relatives. It is the unnamed shadow on an unknown number of death certificates—of handicapped newborns; sickly, aged parents; the terminally ill in critical pain.

No, Debbie's case is something new only because of the public nature of both its telling and the debate that has followed.

This story was first written, anonymously but without apology, by the intern himself, and published in the *Journal of the American Medical Association* (*JAMA*)—one of the most respected medical journals in the world.

Following the article's publication, the commentary came fast and furious. Some experts dismissed the incident as fictional. Others believed it, but focused their criticism on the young doctor's lack of familiarity with Debbie's medical history.

But the article's greatest effect was to yank euthanasia out of the closet and thrust it into the arena of national debate. On the surface that might seem healthy, getting the whole ugly issue into the open. But there's a subtle danger here: The *JAMA* article and the impassioned discussion it provoked offer a case study of a recurring process in American life by which the unthinkable in short order becomes the unquestionable.

Usually it works like this: Some practice so offensive that it could scarcely be discussed in public is suddenly advocated by a respected expert in a respected forum. The public is shocked, then outraged. The very fact that such a thing could be publicly debated becomes the focus of debate.

But in the process the sheer repetition of the shocking gradually dulls its shock effect. No longer outraged, people begin to argue for positions to moderate the extreme; or they accept the premise, challenging instead the means to achieve it. (Note that in Debbie's debate, many challenged not the killing, but the intern's failure to check more carefully into the case.)

And gradually, though no one remembers quite how it all happened, the once unspeakable becomes tolerable and, in time, acceptable.

An example of how this process works is the case of homosexuality. Not long ago it was widely regarded, even in secular society, as a perversion. The gay rights movement's first pronouncements were received with shock; then, in the process of debate, the public gradually lost its sense of outrage. Homosexuality became a cause—and what was once deviant is today, in many jurisdictions, a legally protected right. All this in little more than a decade.

Debbie's story appears to have initiated this process for euthanasia. Columnist Ellen Goodman welcomed the case as "a debate that should be taking place."

So what was once a crime becomes a debate. And if history holds true, that debate will usher the once unmentionable into common practice.

Already the stage is set. In a 1983 poll, 63 percent of Americans approved of mercy killing in certain cases. In a 1988 poll, more than 50 percent of lawyers favored legal euthanasia. The Hemlock Society is working to put the issue on the ballot in several states.

I don't intend to sound alarmist; legal euthanasia in this country is still more a threat than a reality. But twenty years ago who would have thought abortion would one day be a constitutional right, or that infanticide would be given legal protection?

The path from the unmentionable to the commonplace is being traveled with increasing speed in medical ethics. Without some concerted resistance, euthanasia is likely to be the next to make the trip. As Ellen Goodman concluded in her column, "The Debbie story is not over yet, not by a long shot."

Indeed.

Novelist Walker Percy, in *The Thanatos Syndrome*, offers one vision of where such compromising debates on the value of life might take us.

The time is the 1990s. Qualitarian Life Centers have sprung up across the country after the landmark case of *Doe v. Dade*, "which decreed, with solid scientific evidence, that the human infant does not achieve personhood until 18 months." At these centers one can conveniently dispose of unwanted young and old alike.

An old priest, Father Smith, confronts the narrator, a psychiatrist, in this exchange:

"You are an able psychiatrist. On the whole a decent, generous humanitarian person in the abstract sense of the word. You know what is going to happen to you."

"What?"

"You are a member of the first generation of doctors in the history of medicine to turn their backs on the oath of Hippocrates and kill millions of old, useless people, unborn children, born malformed children, for the good of mankind—and to do so without a single murmur from one of you. Not a single letter of protest in the august *New England Journal of Medicine*. And do you know what you are going to end up doing?"

"No," I say . . .

The priest aims his azimuth squarely at me and then appears to lose his train of thought . . .

"What is going to happen to me, Father?" I ask before he gets away altogether.

"Oh," he says absently, appearing to be thinking of something else, "you're going to end up killing Jews."

October 1988

Chapter Ten

A Remedy for Christian "Homophobia": Coercive Enlightenment

Religious liberty has been under relentless assault in recent years. Cases have sought to banish the Ten Commandments from children's classrooms, creches from town greens, and Bible studies from both public schools and private homes. But now, I fear, a new line has been crossed: A District of Columbia court has ordered a Roman Catholic institution to pay the bill for homosexual dance mixers.

The case, which has aroused surprisingly little interest among evangelicals, began eight years ago [1980]. A student organization, the Gay People of Georgetown University (GPGU), demanded recognition and funds from the university in order to sponsor gay social events and promote homosexual education. Georgetown refused, arguing diplomatically that "while it supports and cherishes the individual lives and rights of its students, it cannot subsidize this cause because it would be an inappropriate endorsement for a Catholic university."

GPGU sued, alleging illegal discrimination. It turns out that under the District of Columbia's Human Rights Act, no organization can legally deny benefits to anyone based on "sexual orientation discrimination"—a term it defines as "male or female homosexuality, heterosexuality and bisexuality, by preference or practice."

At the initial hearing, the D.C. Superior Court sided with Georgetown. The court agreed that the general constitutional guarantee of religious freedom took precedence over Washington's Human Rights Act.

GPGU appealed. And in November 1987, the D.C. Court of Appeals reversed the decision, concluding: "The District of Columbia's compelling interest in the eradication of sexual orientation discrimination outweighs any burden imposed upon Georgetown's exercise of religion by the forced equal provision of tangible benefits."

Translated out of legalese, this means the court believes guaranteeing homosexual rights to be so central to government's role that it outweighs the right of religious institutions to distribute their money according to their beliefs. Thus, a local thirteen-member city council was able to pass a simple ordinance arbitrarily determining Washington's "compelling interest"—and, sweeping aside 200 years of established constitutional protections, a local court enforced it.

This is frightening. After all, what government bureaucracy doesn't think its own interest is "compelling"?

The court did affirm that Georgetown need not give formal university recognition to GPGU, acknowledging that it could not determine what the university should *think* about homosexuality (though there is the implication that they would if they could). But it did force the university to further the District's vision of equality by requiring that it finance its gay student organization.

The attitude seems clear, if not stated baldly: "Though your doctrine—to which you are entitled—is backward and unenlightened, at least we can make you behave in a progressive and enlightened fashion." But as constitutional scholar (and Georgetown professor) Walter Berns commented, ". . . what qualified an American court to pass judgment on the validity of a moral teaching?"

Though the decision applies only in the District, it raises disturbing implications.

First, if this type of judicial reasoning prevails, any religious institution will be subject to the same intrusions wherever there happens to be a local anti-discrimination law that includes provisions for homosexuals. If in Illinois, then Wheaton College. If in Virginia, then CBN University. If it becomes part of national civil rights legislation, this religion-bashing could blanket the country.

Second, the decision raises the prospect that other state interests might be accorded similar treatment. The reasoning suggests that any "compelling" government interest outweighs religious interest, no matter what doctrines get trampled. What of the church that ordains no women pastors? Or the Jewish seminary that admits only Jews?

To follow the logic of the D.C. decision, religious freedom is reduced to choosing prayers or humming hymns rather than deciding whom the church can hire or what groups a religious institution can support or fund. Religious institutions can be required by law to reflect every so-called civil rights trend of the moment—at least when it comes to the provision of benefits.

With so much at stake, you would expect Georgetown to appeal to the Supreme Court. Astonishingly, it did not. The university, like a man boasting of the necktie used to hang him, proclaimed the decision a victory. Since the court required the university not to recognize the gay group, just fund it, Georgetown announced it had won an important point, and could therefore give up the fight and set about to heal and rebuild.

Besides, as Georgetown's president wrote foggily in a ten-page letter to alumni, "The University's presence in the delicate area of teaching is needed, but may well also appeal to those to whom it is directed both as an interference and a disputable one at that." (Heaven forbid that the church might call sin "sin" and thus "interfere" with anyone's free choice.)

Maybe Georgetown just suffered from legal exhaustion; granted, it fought the case for eight years. But it is hard to avoid the suspicion that the school caved in to the pressure of "enlightened" opinion. No institution wants to risk appearing to the Washington community as a bastion of homophobia. That's a disease as dreaded among the city's media and political elites as AIDS.

But one thing is clear: Georgetown's surrender in refusing to contest the court's decision has allowed this intrusive legislation to stand for any religious institution in the nation's capital. Landmark court decisions of this type, though not directly binding elsewhere, are often used to support legal arguments in similar cases. They provide a precedent, a model of sorts.

Georgetown contends that it stood its ground, that the court's decision was a partial victory. A few more victories like this and there will be precious little religious liberty left to defend.

July 1988

Chapter Eleven

Spying on Henry Hyde at Mass

Religion, a friend of mine joked, is being treated today the same way homosexuality once was: As long as it is practiced only among consenting adults behind closed doors, it is tolerated.

I thought of this irreverent quip while watching NBC's news coverage of the Supreme Court decision striking down Louisiana's "creation science" law. The counsel who represented Louisiana argued that the legislature was merely seeking to assure equal discussion of equally valid theories regarding the origins of man; academic freedom demanded no less. Anchor Tom Brokaw appeared frustrated. Finally he asked, "But weren't many sponsors of this bill *religious* people doing this for *religious* reasons?"

For Brokaw, apparently a person with religious motivations has no business injecting those into public debate; it seems religious convictions might contaminate public policy.

This shocking attitude is held not just by the American Civil Liberties Union and People for the American Way, but by a lot of otherwise sensible people who have been conditioned into believing that public debate should be free of any religious influence.

The U.S. Supreme Court has encouraged this mind-set. In

1971's *Lemon v. Curtzman*, the Court applied a threefold test of constitutionality: First, a law's primary effect must neither advance nor inhibit religion. Second, it must not result in excessive entanglement of government with religion. Fair enough so far. But the third tenet holds that a law must be adopted with a "secular intent"—and that is where difficulties arise.

It was on this third point, in fact, that the Louisiana law was struck down. The law's drafters expressly stated a secular purpose—balanced academic teaching—but that expressed purpose was held by the Court to be a "sham." Justice Brennan argued bluntly in a majority decision that the sponsor's motivation was religious—hence the law itself was unconstitutional.

My concern here is not to argue the merits of the Louisiana law. It may not have been wisely drafted or advanced true academic freedom. But the grounds on which it was struck down establishes a chilling precedent. If the effect of the Court's decision is to hold that any motivation for passing a law—be it conservatism, liberalism, Marxism, or whatever—is valid *except* religion, then we will have perverted religious freedom into a monstrous form of religious repression.

Congressman Henry Hyde offers a firsthand account of what it means to run afoul of this bigotry. In 1976 Congress passed the Hyde Amendment, which barred federal funding of abortion in the Medicaid program. Planned Parenthood, the ACLU, and other groups challenged the amendment's constitutionality, claiming it imposed "a peculiarly religious view of when a human life begins." To prove their theory, the plaintiffs' lawyers asked to review Hyde's mail for expressions of religious sentiment—such as the suspicious use of "God bless you" at the end of a letter. Their private investigator followed Hyde to a mass for the unborn, covertly making notes as the congressman read Scripture, took Communion, and prayed.

The plaintiffs testified that these observations evidenced a simmering religious conspiracy, claiming that Hyde, a devout Catholic, could not separate his religion from his politics and that the Hyde Amendment was thus unconstitutional.

Planned Parenthood and the ACLU ultimately lost their case. But Hyde later wrote, "Some powerful members of the cultural elites in our country . . . go to Gestapo lengths to inhibit [religious] expression."

The authors of a New York law outlawing the use of children in pornography certainly went to lengths to avoid a legal battle like Hyde's or Louisiana's. In its preamble, the statute specifically states that the law is *not* based on any moral or religious considerations. Only by making such a specific disclaimer did the bill's drafters believe they could avoid a court challenge.

That this bias against religious motivations exists is disturbing enough. But do we really understand where this growing intolerance can lead us—what kind of society we would have if the public square were sanitized of religious values?

The abolition campaign, the reform of inhumane prison and working conditions, child labor laws, education reform, and the civil rights movement: all these sprang from religiously informed motives. What would the history of social justice be like without the likes of William Wilberforce, John Wesley, Lord Shaftesbury, William Jennings Bryan, Martin Luther King? Such leaders were from both the political Left and Right, theological liberals and conservatives alike.

Even such a generally irreligious observer as John Dewey once commented, "The church-going classes, those who have come under the influence of . . . Christianity . . . form the backbone of philanthropic and social interest, of social reform through political action, of pacifism, of popular education. They embody and express the spirit of kindly good will towards [those] in economic disadvantage."

Religiously-motivated political activism brings a transcendent moral perspective to the turmoil of contemporary political affairs. While the separation of the institutions of church and state is a vital constitutional safeguard, no one ever intended the religious and political realms to be separated. To do so is to sterilize our body politic and leave it morally impoverished.

For me, Tom Brokaw's question was hauntingly reminiscent of the celebrated remark of Lord Melbourne in Parliament 200 years ago. Rising in indignation to oppose the abolition campaign led by an outspoken Christian, William Wilberforce, Melbourne thundered, "Things have come to a pretty pass when religion is allowed to invade public life." Had Melbourne prevailed and Wilberforce been disqualified because he spoke his Christian conscience, the abominable slave trade might not have ended.

Two centuries ago the answer to Melbourne's challenge was yes: in the name of humanity and justice, religion must invade public life. The answer to Tom Brokaw's question today should be no less.

November 1987

Chapter Twelve

Private Sins and Public Officials: So What?

When a reporter publicly asked Gary Hart if he had ever committed adultery, an invisible barrier that had shielded political leaders for generations suddenly crumbled. Why are journalists no longer willing to honor their long-established pact to look away from such dalliances? Is the media suddenly displaying a long-repressed strain of Puritan moralism?

Hardly.

The more likely explanation lies with Hart himself. His cavalier invitation for reporters to tail him—"You'll be bored"— was too tempting for any reporter worth his weight in telephoto lenses to resist.

Debate in the aftermath of the Hart monkey business focused not only on the journalistic ethics of lurking in the bushes to catch politicians in the act—or at least the appearance of the act. On that issue the verdict was mixed.

The debate also raised a much more fundamental issue: whether or not the private actions of public officials have public consequences. On this point the verdict was almost unanimous: Private morality is not relevant. Most commentators seemed to shrug off the issue with the modern equivalent of the classic comment, "It doesn't matter what you do in the bedroom as long as you don't do it in the street and frighten the horses."

This response is not surprising, I suppose, in an age that takes its moral lessons from Phil Donahue and Oprah Winfrey.

The question of whether or not private morality is publicly relevant was quickly put to the test in the wake of the Hart stories, when Massachusetts Representative Barney Frank became the first member of the U.S. Congress willingly to acknowledge his homosexuality. "I don't think my sex life is relevant to my job," he told the *Boston Globe*. "But on the other hand I don't want to leave the impression that I'm embarrassed about my life."

Representative Frank concluded, "If you ask the direct question: 'Are you gay?' the answer is: 'Yes. So what?'"

So what?

Well, Frank's bravado would appear to be justified. After all, several years ago one of his most ardent defenders, Representative Gerry Studds, was found to have engaged in a sodomous relationship with a male, teenaged congressional page. Yet his constituents unhesitatingly returned him to office the next year. And a *Boston Globe* poll conducted the weekend of Frank's disclosure revealed that 87 percent believed his homosexuality would make no difference in his campaign. Some even thought his candid disclosures might help him.

So what? I hardly know where to begin.

One of the most fundamental principles of ethics is that moral responsibility in the small things of life is the only reliable preparation for larger tasks. Far from being trivial, minor tests of character are the best basis on which to predict future behavior. A line of Jesus' parable about this principle captures the point: "You have been faithful with a few things; I will put you in charge of many things" (Matthew. 25:21).

But what about those who are already in charge of many things and are unfaithful with personal things? A politician who lacks self-discipline and judgment in his family affairs will lack it in handling the affairs of the nation. It is a matter of character.

And that is only the half of it. Public officials, whether they realize it or not, are also engaged in moral leadership. Sissela Bok of Brandeis University put it this way in *Time*: "Aristotle said that people in government exercise a teaching function. Among other things, we see what they do and think this is how we should act."

Thus governmental officials, by virtue of their authority and visibility, are role models and key arbiters of social values. So when Congressman Frank defends his homosexuality, he attempts to give it moral legitimacy—exactly the wrong message to be sending to a generation of adolescents grappling with their sexual "preference."

But even apart from moral questions, consider the practical effects Frank's comment may have in light of the deadly public health threat called AIDS.

In all the recent attention focused on AIDS, one important fact seems to have been shoved into the closet: Homosexual intercourse has been and remains the principal vehicle for the spread of the disease. Monsignor Eugene Clark writes in *Crisis*, "In fact, the virus-turned-plague has only one source—sodomy. Heterosexuals are infected only from homosexuals, or from heterosexuals infected by bisexuals."

And no matter how fervently Frank may endorse "safe sex," some of his listeners will adopt his "so what?" attitude without the precautions he advocates. Representative Frank is, in short, throwing gasoline on a fire that threatens to incinerate millions. In light of this, can anyone conscionably say, "So what?" to the question whether the private morality of a political leader has any bearing on public consequences?

Certainly public officials will never be moral superheroes. They are bound to sin just like anyone else. But while the social consequences of a doctor admitting adultery or a car dealer coming out of the closet are limited, for a public official the effects are far more widespread. Politicians and public leaders must be held to higher moral standards for the simple reason that they are role models who set standards for others.

Of all the conclusions of the Hart affair—or Barney Frank's

disclosures—none would be more tragic than if we as a nation merely sensationalized the story and missed the lesson. Our leaders' private moral decisions inevitably affect not only their public policy decisions, but the lives of those they lead.

And that can even be a matter of life and death.

August 1987

Chapter Thirteen

What the Sodomy Ruling Really Means

Winston Churchill advised, "If you have an important point to make, don't try to be subtle or clever. Use a pile driver. Hit it once. Then come back and hit it again."

I previously wrote about a crucial debate over the nature of constitutional government. One side, represented by Supreme Court Justice William Brennan, asserts that the Constitution's essential meaning lies in the eye of its judicial beholder; the other, championed by Attorney General Edwin Meese [written in 1986], argues that it is an objective standard as binding on the courts as on other branches of government. At issue is whether the foundation of our legal order rests on judicial subjectivism or original intent.

Here I get out my sledgehammer to drive the point home once more, but now in light of a Supreme Court decision that has brought the debate into clear focus.

In June 1986, the Court, split 5 to 4, handed down one of its most controversial rulings in decades. The subject was bound from the start to draw attention: the government in the bedroom.

In 1982 Georgia police arrested one Michael Hardwick on charges of sodomy. While serving a warrant on an unrelated charge, officers had found Hardwick engaged in sexual relations with another man. Under Georgia law this is a felony punishable by up to twenty years in prison. Though Hardwick was not prosecuted, he challenged the law on the grounds that it violated his right to privacy.

In a ruling that surprised many, the Supreme Court reversed a lower court and upheld the Georgia sodomy statute.

An uproar ensued. Protesters marched in gay communities from Greenwich Village to San Francisco. Political cartoons depicted Supreme Court justices in bed with homosexual couples. A *Newsweek* photo showed two gay protesters in passionate embrace under a placard reading "Supreme Bigotry." The outraged *Washington Post* demanded, "What now? Can we expect an army of police to be assigned to peeping patrol; instructed to barge into bedrooms and arrest anyone who deviates from the most conventional sexual practice?" *Time* moaned that the case was decided "to the delight of religious Fundamentalists and other anti-gays."

At first blush, my libertarian sensibilities were offended as well. The decision conjures up images of policemen breaking down bedroom doors, gun and camera in hand. After all, isn't a man's home his castle?

It is—up to a point. Privacy is a crucial right; but, like all rights, it is not absolute. We do not accept an absolute right to privacy in cases of child abuse, rape, or incest.

Private acts ought generally to be our own business, unless they threaten the rights of other individuals or the public health. George Will writes, "An individual getting regularly drunk on gin may be a private matter. Millions of workers and parents getting regularly drunk on gin is a social disaster—and was a reason for British licensing laws." Likewise, the terrifying AIDS epidemic might well be sufficient reason for the state to intervene in what would otherwise be private affairs.

But the Supreme Court decision had nothing to do with these issues. It makes no judgment as to the wisdom of the Georgia law or any anti-sodomy statute.

The Court simply stated that it could find no constitutional right to sodomy, conduct uniformly outlawed when the Constitution was adopted. States are thus free to regulate—or not to regulate—such conduct without Supreme Court interference. That is all that it said—no more and no less.

But the real significance of this decision has been largely missed by the hysterical media. It has little to do with sexual behavior; it has everything to do with the original intent of the Constitution's framers.

Justice White wrote in the ruling, "The Court is most vulnerable and comes nearest to illegitimacy when it deals with judge-made constitutional law having little or no cognizable roots in the language or design of the Constitution." By creating new, fundamental rights, White argued, "the judiciary necessarily takes to itself further authority to govern the country without express constitutional authority."

In short, the Court ruled that it should not be in the business of creating rights not found in the Constitution. This is the heart of the Meese-Brennan debate.

This decision is thus a direct challenge to sixty years of judicial activism that sought to replace the "jurisprudence of original intention" with a culturally relative, ultimately subjective determination of "essential meaning."

Few have taken notice, but the logic of this ruling, if consistently applied in the future, could dramatically change the direction of the Court. The past decision that could be most directly affected is none other than *Roe v. Wade*, the apogee of judicial activism that legalized abortion-on-demand.

I don't often look to Eleanor Smeal of the National Organization for Women for insightful constitutional commentary. But concerning the sodomy ruling, she is right on the mark: "If *Roe* is ever reversed, this is exactly the way the decision will be written."

To apply the logic of the sodomy case to *Roe v. Wade* is to reverse *Roe v. Wade*. If the language of the Constitution is normative and if the Court has no authority to create new, fundamental rights, the right to abortion "discovered" in 1973 is no more constitutional than the right to sodomy.

The sodomy decision is, in itself, an important one. But its real significance goes much further. If the Court's logic holds, it has sounded the death knell for legalized abortion. And that can come not a day too soon.

September 1986

Chapter Fourteen

Is the Constitution Out of Date?

In this high-tech age, it may not be unfair to compare American journalism with a fast-food restaurant. Every issue, no matter how weighty, is served up in neat packages with catchy labels; an impatient public may get instant gratification but little nourishment.

A good example exists in coverage [1986] of the simmering dispute between Attorney General Edwin Meese and Supreme Court Justice William Brennan over constitutional interpretation.

Mr. Meese championed a "jurisprudence of original intention," meaning that judges should rely on the intent of the document's authors in deciding constitutional questions. Brennan and allies respond that since it is often impossible to discover original intent, judges must determine the Constitution's "essential meaning."

Judging by the thirty-second newsburgers, this is merely another Washington political squabble: a right-wing attorney general out to overturn permissive court decisions, while embattled court liberals defend the rights of the oppressed.

But the news media have missed it altogether. Meese versus Brennan raises fundamental questions about both American government and the values by which we live.

The most obvious relates to the role of the Court. Meese believes that when judges "find" in the Constitution rights and obligations nobody ever put there, they move from interpreting law to making law. As Franklin Roosevelt said, "We want a Supreme Court which will do justice *under* the Constitution—not over it."

Justice Brennan counters that the Court's "power to give meaning" to the Constitution has produced the social progress of the last fifty years. To adopt Meese's "narrow" position, he says, would undo it.

Brennan may be right when he claims the Supreme Court has acted when Congress should have, but did not; desegregation is a good example. But does social expediency warrant the judiciary taking on legislative powers?

The Founding Fathers didn't think so. They understood that the courts, far from being legislators themselves, should serve as restraints on the potentially dangerous passions of the democratic majority. Tocqueville saw this clearly: "Courts of law should act as the final brake upon extremes of popular opinion and should protect the public from their own temporary following after the false gods of extreme sentimentalism and fashionable theorism."

The conflict between Mr. Meese and Mr. Brennan also raises a second, even more crucial question: What is the nature of law itself?

From a Christian perspective, law has always been understood as an attempt, however incomplete, to reflect God's objective order in the universe. Moses and his appointed judges sought to administer judgment not according to some arbitrary notion of fairness, but according to an objective standard of justice.

The Constitution framers inherited this same tradition from Reformation philosophy: *lex rex*, which holds that law, based on objective truth, rules over man. In writing the Constitution, the founders assumed the existence of an objective body of principles, largely Judeo-Christian in origin, that would serve as the foundation for the legal framework of the new nation. For two centuries this value consensus has served to legitimize the law.

In contending that law must be interpreted in this historical framework, Mr. Meese is not simply a hidebound traditionalist, as he is often portrayed. Rather, he is arguing that law must be based on moral authority, not on sociological expediency. The choice that he presents is a stark one. At the bottom line, law not supported by moral authority can be enforced only at the point of a bayonet.

In arguing that law rests on absolutes—which presupposes there *are* absolutes—Mr. Meese is exposing a raw nerve in this relativistic age. Among other things, he is challenging the belief that since there is no objective truth, human language has no objective meaning. Extremists of this position champion what one Yale law professor has called "critical legal studies," the rather cheerless proposition that since words have no objective meaning, neither do laws—or the Constitution.

This mind-set is alien to the Christian who believes that a sovereign God created man with a capacity to understand unchanging truth conveyed in human terms. Human language is thus God's ordained instrument for communicating truth.

One of the ironies of the current debate is that Mr. Brennan argues that his view best protects minorities. True, recent liberal court decisions may have helped the poor and powerless. But that is a consequence of the convictions particular judges have brought to the bench—not a result of the system Brennan advocates. In fact, the judicial subjectivism he advances would do just the opposite. When skepticism about meaning infects our legal system, all "brakes upon extremes of popular opinion" give way. Should popular opinion shift, the tyranny of unrestrained majority passion is inflicted first upon the powerless. The rule of law affords the only certain protection of the individual.

We will be indebted to Messrs. Meese and Brennan if their ongoing debate causes us to reexamine the peculiar nature of our Constitution. It is not historic free verse, the interpretation of which lies in the eye of the beholder. It took its shape 200 years ago out of the radical idea that men could band together to be governed not by a monarchy, but by their own social compact. The Constitution was the contract between the people and the government they established.

Today the issue before us is whether we continue to honor the terms of the contract—whether our society holds itself accountable to transcendent values, or regards its laws as merely subjective.

At root that is a religious question. As Washington pastor Myron Augsburger reminds us, the church's duty is "to hold government morally accountable before God to live up to its own claims." The church must be the conscience of America's social contract.

We Christians should thus be parties of first interest in Meese versus Brennan.

August 1986

Chapter Fifteen

Terrorism's "Catch-22"

Terrorism provided 1985's most unforgettable images: the Moslem hijacker holding a pistol to the head of TWA Captain John Testrake; the fresh grave at Arlington Cemetery of young Robert Stethem; the widow of Leon Klinghoffer weeping at his funeral;. the wreckage of bombings from Belfast to Beirut.

It was high drama, as TV provided instant coverage. Then, as each crisis passed, the coverage abruptly ended, as if it were simply another TV miniseries. Americans returned to daily routines, government to more pressing issues.

But terrorism is more than TV drama; it has emerged in the eighties as the greatest single threat to world stability. According to *U.S. News and World Report*, there are now ten incidents per day, up from ten per week in 1970. More than 140 terrorist bands operate in fifty countries—succeeding 91 percent of the time!

So there is a far better chance for political success these days with a bomb than a ballot. Any madman can get worldwide, instant exposure for any cause, courtesy of high-tech satellites and compliant TV editors. Thus dramatic incidents such as TWA's Flight 847 and the takeover of the Italian cruise ship *Achille Lauro* are, I fear, but a portent of things to come.

So it is time for the nation and the Christian community to grapple with some of the painful questions forced upon us by the age of terror.

To do so we must first understand the nature of today's terrorist.

According to *U.S. News and World Report*, he is typically twenty to twenty-three years old, unmarried, from a middle- or upper-class urban family, and driven by the kind of hatred, as Che Guevara described it, that "push[es] a human being . . . and makes him a cold, violent, selective, and effective killing machine."

The terrorist's victim is often part of the establishment, but violence must be shocking and random, so anyone is fair game.

According to the *Minimanual of the Urban Guerrilla*, a guidebook widely distributed among terrorists, what matters is not the identity of their corpse but its impact on their audience. Violence is thus used deliberately and dispassionately, carefully engineered for *theatrical effect.*

Small wonder that TV is such a popular medium for terrorist acts!

The terrorist's strategy is calculated to force governments into an impossible dilemma. To preserve order in the face of violence, governments may be forced to restrict individual freedoms. But such restrictions can be perceived by the populace as repression, which in turn incites revolt. Yet if a government does nothing in the face of terrorist attack, fear and anarchy reign.

Thus, whether the government attacked responds by doing nothing or by restricting personal freedoms, in either case its ineffectiveness is made apparent. And the terrorist wins.

This was dramatically illustrated in the aftermath of the *Achille Lauro* hijacking.

In the controversy following its failure to detain Palestine Liberation Front leader Abul Abbas, the Italian government crumbled. So while the bandits failed in their announced mission to free Palestine Liberation Organization prisoners, they succeeded in another even more strategic objective, the collapse of a Western ally's government.

Even military retaliation can play into this Catch-22 dilemma. As one Shiite leader boasted during the TWA crisis, "[A]nything that America carries out will make the peoples of the region anti-American and this is a basic victory for us."

Traditional responses simply don't work in the age of terrorism. How can we then combat its evils?

First, we must face reality: Today's political terrorism amounts to open warfare. For the most part, these are not random acts of violence, but the actions of a well-financed network of those who, for one reason or another, want to destroy the West.

Western governments will eventually have to respond accordingly. That may mean stricter security and more effective intelligence, military force against terrorist headquarters, and crippling economic sanctions against countries that export terrorism. It can also mean offensive action, as the U.S. roundup of the *Achille Lauro* hijackers well demonstrates.

But actions like these raise painful ethical dilemmas for Christians.

If terrorism is indeed war, then what is the Christian's response? Though I respect my brethren who are pacifists, I cannot share their views. Government is Biblically ordained to preserve order, which may require the use of force to restrain evil.

Living in a fallen world often requires choosing the lesser of two evils, accepting the reality that some evils have consequences more harmful than others. The U.S. seizure of the Egyptian airliner—admittedly air piracy—was an "evil" justified to prevent a greater evil of allowing perpetrators of international crimes to escape justice.

At the same time—and there is a tension here—Christians are to be a leavening influence. We can endorse only that force which is absolutely necessary for government to preserve order. And we must not allow order to be purchased at the expense of liberty.

In addition, as Christians we must seek to interpret current events in light of God's revelation in Scripture. Could it be that He is using this ragged crew of outlaws to shatter our idolatrous reliance on government and human institutions to provide ultimate stability? All the high-tech military might of our much-vaunted civilization is impotent against suicidal zealots in explosive-laden trucks.

Or could it be, as Paul wrote to the Romans, that God is simply abandoning us to our own sin? We should not be surprised to find ourselves plagued by gratuitous bloodshed when for years we have enjoyed a glut of violence as entertainment. We may be falling victim in real life to that which we have vicariously exalted on the screen.

I pray not. But we must confront the hard questions. Do Western governments have the capacity to fulfill their Biblically ordained role to preserve order? Does Western culture have the moral reserve to confront barbarism while preserving its civility?

We Christians must speak to these issues—or one day be held to account for our silence.

January 1986

PART II

Culture

Chapter Sixteen

Secular Orthodoxy and
Other Oxymorons

Marc Christian, former live-in lover of Rock Hudson, recently sued Mr. Hudson's estate because the late actor didn't tell him he had AIDS. And though Mr. Christian has tested negative for the fatal disease, he has also won big: A California court awarded him $14.5 million in damages.

Ironic: This is the same state that enforces regulations forbidding health insurance companies from testing potential policyholders for AIDS, a policy endorsed by the California Medical Association.

So, on the one hand homosexuals' right to privacy is protected—even to the extent that they can get insurance, while patients with cardiac disease or tuberculosis cannot. On the other hand, the estate of a practicing homosexual was held liable for his failure to disclose his AIDS.

This is odd, of course, but perhaps not that unusual in today's schizophrenic society. Take, for instance, a similar inconsistency at work on the environmental front, as pointed out by Mark Rentz, an Arizona State University English professor, in the December 1988 issue of *Chronicles* magazine.

Rentz has observed that evolutionists used to be purists who said that man and Nature were the result of "the impersonal plus time plus chance." According to their Darwinian worldview, the fittest survive, the less fit do not.

But many of today's environmentalists wring their hands over endangered species like condors and snail darters. Darwin would respond to them—if he had survived, that is—that the strong will thrive. If the condor can't adapt to the California freeways (who can blame him), then that's his problem.

(And as Rentz points out without subtlety: "The California condor is . . . ugly, feeds on carrion, has a cue-ball head . . . and vomits whenever it is mildly frightened. This is one bird that is clearly a result of the impersonal plus time plus chance. Why get choked up about its demise?")

But people care about condors and elephants and eagles. Those who claim to be Darwin's disciples but become personally involved with the beauty, order, and purpose of Nature seem to long for something more than natural selection and random collisions of atoms and primal slime.

"The evolutionist who believes nature, and man, is purposeful, moral, inherently beautiful, and important will find himself at odds with every jot and tittle of evolutionary theory . . . the compassionate or sentimental evolutionist is nothing more than a scientific oxymoron," concludes Rentz.

Perhaps the most dismaying evidence of this secular oxymoron in action comes in the abortion issue.

In India, the widespread use of amniocentesis has allowed couples to know the sex of their child before birth, resulting in thousands of female abortions. In India, girls are a tremendous economic burden to their parents. One study revealed that out of 8,000 Bombay abortions, 7,999 involved a female fetus.

Feminists all over the world rightly decry this barbaric practice. But for the wrong reason. They oppose the "selective" abortion of girls as "female feticide." Yet they affirm the abortion of male and female fetuses as "a woman's right to choose."

It seems that those who worship at the altar of reproductive choice do so when a pregnant woman uses retardation, convenience, birth control, or economics to make her decision for abortion. But if her choice is based on a lack of desire to bear a female baby, then the pro-choicers are up in arms.

Inconsistencies, such as pro-choicers against choice, sentimental evolutionists, and states that at the same time affirm and deny homosexual rights to privacy, abound in our secular culture. It's not hard to understand why: Standards of right and wrong, based on a belief in absolute truth, have all but vanished. Relativism reigns, and pragmatism is its offspring; moral decisions are made on the basis of what works.

But what infuriates me is the smug moralism that those who advance such positions adopt. Relativists have no proper claim to values of "moral" and "immoral." As R. C. Sproul says, their values are "preferences rather than principles."

For pro-choice feminists to argue the "immorality" of female feticide is so illogical that they should be laughed right out of the debate. They can hold their murderous views if they like, and be prepared to pay the price. But they shouldn't wander about spreading vague and self-righteous drivel about defending female fetuses.

In spite of how much they irk us, however, these inconsistencies should encourage rather than discourage Christians. For they expose the absurdity of much secular thought. So often nonbelievers disdain us as anachronists clinging to an ancient orthodoxy with no relevance for the modern world. Well, it is far better to cling to an ancient orthodoxy, with its firm standard of truth, than to claim no orthodoxy at all, yet still act as if you have one.

Today's secularists argue their views with such vehemence that one would assume they wait on the wisdom of the ages—when in reality they waft on the whim of the moment. And we who are Christians have a grand opportunity to point out, as Francis Schaeffer put it so well, that they have "both feet firmly planted in midair."

June 1989

Chapter Seventeen

Art on the Offensive

They say one person's trash is another's treasure. Congress has recently considered government funding for works of art that have been called both. Senator Jesse Helms, for one, had no doubt. The photography in question, he said, is "immoral trash." Helms proposed a congressional ban on the use of public money to disseminate "obscene or indecent materials" or materials that would blaspheme religion.

For his efforts Senator Helms was pilloried in the media. *New York Times* columnist Tom Wicker labeled him "Senator Know-Nothing." Others called Helms a mindless, indecent bigot.

But the vitriol spewed upon the senator reveals more about the levels of tolerance of the Tom Wickers of our day than the alleged intolerance of Jesse Helms.

You are probably well-acquainted with the origins of this controversy: the $45,000 subsidies given by the National Endowment for the Arts to the work of photographers Robert Mapplethorpe and Andres Serrano.

Mapplethorpe, who died of AIDS in March 1989, has been called "one of the preeminent photographers of his generation." But some of Mapplethorpe's subject matter is less eminent: such images as oral sex between lesbian lovers; two men in black leather and the paraphernalia of bondage and torture, one urinating into the other's mouth; photographs of naked children.

The other funded photographer, Andres Serrano, is best known for his work depicting a crucifix submerged in a flask of urine.

These images are not just the private, torturous expressions of their creators. Federal funds supported Mapplethorpe's and Serrano's projects: your tax dollars at work. Hence the public and congressional outcry against the National Endowment for the Arts.

It should be noted that the NEA did not self-consciously decide to promote homosexual sadomasochism or blasphemy. The agency, which dispensed 156.3 million dollars in grants last year, was rather the victim of its own bureaucratic ineptitude. Serrano was funded by what the NEA calls a "regrant": money was given to an intermediary group, which in turn funded him. An NEA spokesperson was quick to acknowledge this work as offensive.

Senator Helms's proposal, designed to prevent this from happening again, was watered down in a procedural move that spared his colleagues from a roll-call vote. (Let me note that in the wave of anti-Helms anger sweeping the art world before the congressional action, a Phoenix art center funded by the National Endowment for the Arts expressed its disdain by displaying the work of an artist known as Cactus Jack: a photograph of Mr. Helms immersed in a jar of urine. Such scurrility deserves no response.)

I applaud Senator Helms's courage in speaking plainly for the millions of Americans offended by art that depicts homosexual sadomasochism or blasphemy.

But I also applaud the right of artists to produce what they will. Government cannot serve as a censor; this is a free country, not a police state. I defend Mr. Serrano's First-Amendment right to create work that patently offends me. But he has no right to do so at my expense. Objecting to paying for that which desecrates one's deeply held religious and moral beliefs is not censorship.

The slings and arrows of outraged artists and columnists hurled against Senator Helms reveal something more than a concern over the stifling of artistic creativity. It reveals a double standard: The outcry today over art and censorship and tolerance depends on whose ox is being gored and whose sensibilities are being offended.

Consider for reference the recent Supreme Court decision regarding the public display each Christmas of a creche in Allegheny, Pennsylvania. The High Court ruled that the creche violates the constitutional ban on state establishment of religion. Justices writing for the majority explained that religious symbols on public property implicitly exclude and offend those who don't adhere to that same religion.

Now, this creche was bought with private funds, not tax dollars. But those offended by Christian symbols applauded the Court's decision as an appropriate recognition of their sensitivities.

No doubt these are the same folk who a few weeks later smeared Senator Helms as a know-nothing bigot. These alleged proponents of tolerance who insist that Christians' tax dollars fund art depicting a crucifix submerged in urine would scream in outrage if the tables were turned and their tax dollars were used to subsidize religious art. They howled about the Christmas creche even though their monies weren't used to fund it.

Among certain defenders of creative expression and societal elites, it seems the only way Christian symbols are acceptable is if they are doused in urine.

November 1989

Chapter Eighteen

Save the Wails

You remember the whales: those three poor, cold, gray mammals in Barrow, Alaska, that brought the civilized world to its knees for two weeks during the 1988 U.S. presidential election.

Trapped by early freezing during their annual migration south, the whales were noticed by Eskimo fishermen, who sounded the alarm—and network executives, looking for a break from the dismal bilge of the presidential campaign, sent 5,000 reporters to Alaska. And it was these unlucky correspondents, swaddled in layers of long johns, some wearing fur-trimmed parkas made from some other innocent animals that nobody even mentioned, who presented the whale tale to the rest of us.

Night after night we witnessed the woes of the whales, heard their tortured breathing as they surfaced in their narrow, icy air holes. We mourned as the smallest of the three finally succumbed and made his way to whale heaven. We held our collective breath as helicopters dropped huge cement blocks through the ice to break a pathway of breathing holes to the sea. Skeptics worried we would kill the whales rather than rescue them.

Then, in their continuing efforts to break the ice in U.S. relations, the Soviets came to the rescue in a massive icebreaker.

Well, after some anxious moments the whales managed to make their way to the open sea. I assume they are safely vacationing somewhere off the coast of Mexico, drinking plankton margaritas and toasting the Soviets. We'll probably never see them again unless they show up as guests on the "Geraldo Rivera Show."

Since the celebrated Alaskan case, I've started a whale file. In it is the Associated Press story about the Austrian tourist who was fined $1,500 after pleading guilty to harassing whales off the coast of Hawaii.

A man named Peter Gottwald sailed to a protected area in ocean waters near Maui to get a good look at the whales who hang out there. I'm not sure just who reported Gottwald, but the U.S. magistrate who fined him sputtered in ire, "It seems perfectly clear that he was chasing the whales. Were he a U.S. citizen, he would spend several nights in jail."

Poor Mr. Gottwald concluded wistfully, "This is not the aloha spirit."

You can imagine my horror. Here I am, pouring my life into prison ministry and criminal justice reforms. Prisons across the country are extremely overcrowded—and now here is a federal magistrate trying to use up scarce prison cells for whale molesters. Fine them if you like, beat them severely with wet blubber, but please don't put them in jail. What will it do to our national statistics and to whales' well-being the world over if they recidivate?

Drawn in by now, I started staying up late poring over animal press clippings. My wife, Patty, who stuck with me through Watergate, for the first time began to worry. She even shipped our goldfish, Pinky, off to the vet for her own protection.

I have expanded my study from those who blubber over whales to those who will do so over just about any animal. I've discovered that animal-rights groups consider bacon and eggs the "breakfast of cruelty." I had long realized that bacon required a pig's ultimate commitment, but had assumed chickens somehow got over the loss of their potential children.

Not so. Losing their eggs produces a severe postpartum depression in impressionable chickens; some have even been known to commit poultricide by standing in heavy rains with their beaks uptilted till they drown.

Some ten million Americans contribute to animal-rights groups whose goals range from protection of endangered species to the banning of woolen clothing because sheep are sometimes nicked in the shearing process.

We have all heard stories of the Animal Liberation Front's break-ins at medical labs in order to free laboratory animals.

And recently a group stormed a Chinese restaurant in Maryland, liberated six lobsters from their holding tank, spirited them to the Maine coast, and set them free.

From whales to chickens and pigs and their parts, it seems there's a lot of emotion and eloquence expended on animal issues these days. I guess I hadn't noticed; I had been preoccupied with caged people rather than animals.

The furor leaves me with two thoughts, however.

One: I hope that the fearsome silliness of animal-rights extremists won't deter us from recognizing our responsibility before God to be good stewards of our environment. We must exercise compassion and wisdom in how we care for our planet and the beasts that fill it. Not because animals have "rights," but because such care is consistent with the human dignity and character to which God calls us.

And second: caring for our furry friends and rescuing trapped whales are indeed worthy causes. But the enormous effort in Alaska, which cost millions of dollars and untold man-hours, is a tragic picture of our often-misplaced priorities as a people.

At the same time those trapped whales were headlining the evening news each night, homeless people huddled on street corners and grates across America. Abused and hungry children went to bed fearful and neglected. Hopeless young men and women were trapped in our inner cities.

The point is simple: Characteristically, Americans have big hearts. We throw ourselves into emergency efforts and expend our energies unreservedly on pet causes.

That is all well and good. But should not at least similar outpourings of compassion, money, time, and energy be expended in sustained, daily effort to help people in need?

July 1989

Chapter Nineteen

Society's Double Standard

In 1988 we heard a passionate outcry over shadows cast on the character of yet another public figure. It wasn't a politician or a pastor this time, however, but an artist whose music both shaped and reflected a generation.

A new unauthorized biography by Albert Goldman painted former Beatle John Lennon as an anorexic, drugged-out bisexual whose last years were characterized by degrading and bizarre behavior. And in response a howl of outrage sounded through Hollywood.

"Entertainment Tonight" featured Lennon apologist Geraldo Rivera reflecting fondly on the "John Lennon I knew" while sadly shaking his rather large head in horror that anyone would dare besmirch such a musical genius. Yoko Ono and friends told their side of the story in *Imagine*, a gentle film tribute to the creativity and vision of their hero. Citing Goldman's book as an example, *Newsweek* pontificated on the larger issue of today's genre of tell-all biographies, musing, "are biographers throwing out the rule book?"

How ironic that this outrage over John Lennon's biography

should come at the very time Hollywood was busily reinventing and in the process desecrating the life of Jesus Christ.

I refer, of course, to Martin Scorsese's *The Last Temptation of Christ*.

I'm not raising *The Last Temptation* simply to beat an already well-beaten film that, after all, will soon fade into well-deserved oblivion on the racks of video rental stores. No, I raise it because Scorsese's film reveals a persistent pattern in our supposedly tolerant American society, and the recent outcry over desecrating poor John Lennon shows up that double standard all too clearly.

Let me explain.

Critics called *The Last Temptation of Christ* such noble things as "serious," "sincere," "breathtaking," "spiritually challenging." Director Scorsese defended the film as his own earnest spiritual pilgrimage to draw him closer to Christ. Why he would want to get closer to the Christ of the film—a wacked-out, lustful, and confused wimp who says, "Lucifer is inside of me"—is a mystery to me. But Scorsese is responsible for what he has created. Blasphemy.

Many Christians marched in protest, made calls, wrote letters, and boycotted Universal Studios. One Christian leader even offered to buy the film for $10 million so he could destroy it—which in turn brought screeches of protest about censorship and First-Amendment rights.

But the First Amendment furor misses the issue. We have no civil means to ban the movie. Unlike England, our nation no longer has blasphemy laws on the books. Scorsese has every legal right to make this terrible film.

He has every *legal* right. But he has violated an unwritten law. For what the U.S. also has are strongly held standards and stigmas against those who would defame or denigrate others.

There are plenty of recent examples of society's outrage when these standards are violated. Consider Al Campanis, long-time executive of the Los Angeles Dodgers, who was summarily dismissed because he made public comments about blacks that were considered offensive. Or Jimmy the Greek, fired from CBS for the same reason. Or the outrage of lawmakers on Capitol Hill as they decried Japan's tolerance of Black Sambo manikins in a Tokyo department store.

But in *The Last Temptation of Christ* we have a free-wheeling, scurrilous, and scabrous attack on the character of Jesus Christ. And Hollywood gurus who would faint dead away if a similar movie was made about Martin Luther King or Gandhi or, of course, John Lennon defend the film in the name of artistic freedom.

This selective tolerance is indicative of a widespread attitude in America today. Plainly said, it's Christian-bashing. Every other group, from homosexuals to Hari Krishnas, is afforded protection from prejudice, lampooning, or being depicted unfairly. If these lines are crossed, the ever-vigilant press sends up a howl of outrage. As they should.

But Christians enjoy no such protection. We are caricatured and parodied—our faith the butt of jokes and its practice the target of lawsuits. And now this—the ultimate attack: painstakingly filmed and scripted sleaze about Jesus.

And if we dare to cry out in protest, the media righteously gather their First-Amendment skirts about them with a sort of cultured and collective disdain, portraying us as intolerant extremists. But where's the tolerance for our views of the sanctity of the God-man we worship as Lord?

The same folks who are so outraged—and rightly so—when slurs offend other Americans vigorously defend Hollywood's right to perpetuate religious slurs that offend millions of Christians. That's a double standard enough to cause them shame—even by Hollywood's standards.

At the height of the Beatles' success in the sixties, John Lennon effused, "We're more popular than Jesus now!" At the time his hubris provoked outrage among Christians. But Lennon was simply observing a fact of modern culture—a truth that has, sadly, grown more evident with the passage of time.

November 1988

Chapter Twenty

Whose Ethics?

In the summer of 1989 everything seemed to fall to pieces on Capitol Hill. The Speaker of the House of Representatives resigned in the face of sixty-nine counts of ethical violations; the House Whip quit rather than endure an investigation into his alleged wrongdoings; and an Ohio congressman was convicted of having sex with a minor. Volleys of ethical accusations and counter-accusations reverberated throughout the Capitol, holding government business hostage in the process.

One business Congress did handle, however, was the bailout of the savings and loan industry, which had been looted by hundreds of unscrupulous operators—a "$150 billion calamity," according to the *Washington Post*. And in testimony before congressional committees came the news that Housing and Urban Development agents had for years skimmed millions from HUD real-estate sales—as *Time* put it, a massive giveaway not to the needy but the greedy.

Meanwhile, out on the street—Wall Street, that is—was junk bond king Michael Milken, who made more than one billion dollars in salary, indicted for securities fraud.

The scandal epidemic has led everyone from fundamentalist

preachers to Norman Lear, who has established a foundation to study business ethics, to agree that the nation is floundering in an ethical swampland. Stand on any soapbox today and passionately cry, "What our nation needs is *ethics*!" and you will be heartily cheered.

But what no one seems to realize is that while we all want ethics, ethics are meaningless unless based on some value system. And the problem is, our society cannot agree on common objective values on which common ethical standards must be based.

This dilemma was illustrated at one of our great academic institutions, where John Shad, former chairman of the Securities and Exchange Commission, donated $35 million to the Harvard Business School to establish an ethics department.

That was two years ago [1987]. And while we assume Harvard has given it the old college try, at this writing it seems that the university has only come up with one rather flimsy-sounding "values" course; otherwise, Harvard is still sitting on the Shad grant, unable to find an ethicist to head up the department.

The quandary was well expressed by Harvard president Derek Bok in an article in *Harvard Magazine* (May/June 1988). Bok describes Harvard's origins: After the school was expanded from a training ground for ministers to include other students, Massachusetts law mandated that "the president [and] the professors . . . shall exert their best endeavors to impress on the minds of youth committed to their care and instruction the principles of piety and justice and a sacred regard for truth."

Bok speaks almost wistfully of returning to such absolutes by which to formulate ethical decisions. But he hastens to note that faculty members react "with tepid interest and outright skepticism" to the idea of teaching any kind of ethics.

So, concludes Bok, an ethics course today "seeks not to convey a set of moral truths but tries to encourage students to think carefully about complex moral issues . . . not to impart 'right answers,' but to make students more perceptive to ethical problems when they arise."

In the absence of "moral truths," Bok reaches the only conclusion he can: He outlines an idea of ethics, but leaves the question of whose ethics will be adopted wholly unanswered. He tries to raise an ethical standard, but he has no flag to fly upon it.

Harvard's problem parallels that of our society at large. Our nation demands ethics, but abandons the objective moral base on which any real standard of ethics must logically rest. Our society deplores the proliferation of scandals, yet rejects the basis for an ethical code designed to restrain the human passions that cause those scandals.

This paradoxical, pathetic attitude brings to mind the image of a starving man at a banquet who refuses the meal that will save his life, simply because it is not to his taste.

The life-and-death truth of the matter is this: Ethics cannot exist in a vacuum. If ethics are relative—the eighties' version of the sixties' pop "situational ethics"—then who is to assert one ethical standard as superior to another? In an age that celebrates tolerance as its supreme virtue, no absolute standard of right and wrong—which by definition excludes other standards—can be adopted. Nor can any satisfactory code of ethics.

If a consensus in our society really wants ethics on Capitol Hill, on Wall Street, in the worlds of business and academia, we must be willing to base those ethics on a firm foundation. And in Western civilization that foundation has been twenty-three centuries of accumulated wisdom, natural law, and the Judeo-Christian tradition based on Biblical revelation.

Until we look again to these classic sources, Harvard will continue to waste both its $35 million and the hearts and minds of its students; Capitol Hill will continue to be a playground for opportunists rather than a place of service for statesmen; and our culture at large, loosed from any absolute foundations of morality, will continue to drift helplessly in a moral quagmire, all the while pitifully pontificating about the loss of ethics.

October 1989

Chapter Twenty-one

The Disney Credo

When I wrote a column assailing the Easter Bunny, I was flooded with letters denouncing me as a grinch. Having sufficiently recovered, I now feel bold enough to challenge an icon even more dear to American sensibilities: Mickey Mouse.

In 1987 I made my first pilgrimage to Walt Disney World. Patty and I spent three days being towed from Fantasy Land to Tomorrow Land and back again by our six-year-old grandson. Charlie sported a Goofy hat, complete with ears and buck teeth. I narrowly escaped being forced to wear a pair of Mickey Mouse ears emblazoned in gold across the back with "Chuck."

But on to the cause of my distress: Certainly I have no desire to assault America's favorite playground, a dazzling showcase of creativity and imagination. But as our days there unfolded, I was struck by two observations.

First, no one around me—and there were lots of people around me—seemed happy. Fathers who had probably saved all year to afford transportation, lodging, food, and entry tickets spent a good deal of time arguing with their spouses, yanking tired children through interminable lines, and surreptitiously checking their watches to see how long until closing time.

Granted, it was August in central Florida: hot, muggy, and every foot of park space filled with sweaty fellow tourists. But the crowds seemed to be rushing from amusement to amusement, feverishly checking off attractions seen against those still to be seen. One flushed mother mopped her child's sticky face while barking at her husband, "Awright!—Now how many more to go?"

Driven in the pursuit of pleasure, they were miserable.

Watching the unsmiling crowds, I was reminded of a young woman profiled in *Psychology Today*. Counseled to give up the endless round of parties, drugs, sex, and alcohol that was driving her into despair, she gasped to her psychiatrist, "You mean I don't have to do everything I want to do?"

On this point, of course, the wonderful world of Disney is but a mirror of the world at large, which tends to exhaust itself on the mistaken notion that multiplying pleasures produces happiness.

My second observation was even more troubling. After a day of Mr. Toad, Tiki Tiki birds, and "It's a Small World" relentlessly ringing in my ears, I was ready for the wonders of Epcot Center, Disney's tribute to humanity's accomplishments.

Inside Epcot's famed "Spaceship Earth" we were treated to the history of human civilization. Before our eyes, man discovered the wheel, Rome fell, the printing press was invented. It was uplifting, exhilarating—except that this selective presentation omitted any reference to man's spiritual history. Christianity, Judaism, and Islam, the world's three major religions, were ignored completely, barring one quick mention of monks who passed written history down for generations to follow.

Other exhibits were similarly selective. Energy, we were told, originated from "the pure radiance of the sun, giving rise to the first stirrings of life—microscopic plants." I asked a spokesperson if this meant all life came from the sun. "Oh, we're just concentrating on energy here," he explained. "The Living Seas exhibit deals more with the origins of life in general."

I resolutely made my way to the Living Seas building. The theater darkened; I watched as the molten Earth was incubated by the sun and then spawned volcanos, which yielded vapors, clouds, and condensation. A sprinkling of rain, then torrents. "The Deluge," intoned the narrator. Thus the seas were born, and in them, life itself—"tiny, single-cell plants—plankton—capturing the energy of the sun . . ." This "seems to say life on Earth began in the ocean," a spokesperson asserted as I winced. "But," he added quickly, "[the filmmakers] aren't committing themselves. They don't like to do anything controversial—especially if there aren't a lot of facts to back it up."

Further exhibits on technology, transportation, and science sparkled with human ability to conquer any frontier. Yet the person of the world of Epcot is evidently a two-dimensional being, for nowhere in Disney's grand tributes to mind, body, and science is there to be found even a passing reference to the human spirit.

It is a curious omission. Is it realistic—or even intellectually honest—to present humanity and the world apart from the great dynamic of history, which is at root spiritual? How does one understand the tragedies of the twentieth century, for example, without examining our greatest dilemma, knowing our own nature?

Yet I pressed on in my exploration, even to the point of waiting an hour and a half to get into "Captain EO." For the uninformed, "Captain EO" is the 3-D fantasy featuring pop star Michael Jackson as a crusader against the wiles of an evil queen, personified as a spider. Patty and I prayed we would see no one we knew as we donned purple 3-D glasses and the special-effects movie began. Charlie squirmed with delight between us.

And there I realized that Disney World's humanistic paradise is not without its own messiah: Michael Jackson, dressed in white, who by the power of his music supernaturally transforms both the evil spider and her henchmen into agents of light.

Far be it from me to denigrate Michael Jackson, that androgynous boy-girl-child-man who recently issued this oddly messianic statement of his mission: "I was sent forth for the world, for the children. But have mercy, for I've been bleeding for a long time now."

Jackson's Epcot performance and the breathtaking special effects were marvelous entertainment for all the kids, myself included. But "Captain EO" capped off my visit to the world of Disney. I'll return in a few years, when I've recovered and my next grandchild has come of age. And I'll enjoy it, as she will.

But we will do so, I pray, with no illusions. The Magic Kingdom, glorious as it is, is but a toy that mirrors this broken world. It ignores, even obscures, the ultimate reality—the enduring Kingdom where God, not humankind, reigns.

February 1988

Chapter Twenty-two

Truth and Consequences

"The God that holds you over the pit of hell, much as one holds a spider or some loathsome insect over the fire, abhors you and is dreadfully provoked . . . you hang by a slender thread with the flames of divine wrath flashing about it . . ."

Jonathan Edwards's legendary sermon, "Sinners in the Hands of an Angry God," was not spoken with fiery passion. Edwards stood motionless as he read his sermon in a monotone from a thick manuscript. But his words electrified his Connecticut congregation. Women screamed aloud; grown men cowered in their pews.

Convicted, Edwards's listeners repented. Revival spilled through the New England valleys into all of the colonies. Fear of ultimate consequences—the judgment of God—led thousands to holy living.

But in the twentieth century notions like the "wrath of God" have been dismissed as the product of Puritan prudery. Right and wrong are no longer moral absolutes to live by, but psychological hang-ups to be healed.

Modern relativism thus ushered in the glorious new age of freedom. Consider how a popular women's magazine has described it:

> Modern technology (and the law of the land) . . . churned out a few things. . . . The Pill . . . You could have sex with an entire army and nothing would happen . . . legalized abortion. No one on earth ever loved having an abortion, but if there was a slip-up . . . you could do something about it and not be accused of a crime. And so we were free!

And there was little concern for the *ultimate* consequences of what used to be known as sin in Edwards's day. By the sixties and seventies the concept of God's judgment was rendered impotent. God was as relative as moral standards—He was dead, perhaps; or too all-loving to punish; or whatever we conceived Him to be. At any rate, He was irrelevant to morality, and that meant fornication, adultery, perversion, and all those other old-fashioned words became rights instead of wrongs.

But in the mid-eighties [written in 1986] the freedom of the sixties and seventies seems to have soured. "The evidence is accumulating that we have passed through an Age of Liberation and are now in an Age of Restraint," editorializes Michael Barone in *The Washington Post*. "Statistics on sexual behavior, consumption habits, and social behavior all show this trend."

Barone's evidence: the steady increase of female teenage premarital intercourse has leveled off; syphilis is down from peaks of a few years ago; the number of abortions has dropped; liquor, wine, and beer sales are slipping; though marijuana statistics aren't reliable, there are indications that use is declining.

Why these sudden changes in lifestyle? Is there a new morality sweeping America, as in Edwards's time?

Cosmopolitan, the glossy women's magazine that elevated

hedonism to new heights in the mid-sixties, offers one explanation. A recent article, titled "The New Chastity," cites the young woman who confesses she has slept with only one man. Why? Because the girl explains matter-of-factly, "I don't want to die."

Her fear is not unfounded. Authorities at the Centers for Disease Control estimate that in the United States there are between 500,000 and one million carriers—both men and women—of AIDS.

Thus the editor of the *Journal of the American Medical Association* wrote recently, "It may behoove those people who do not wish to get AIDS to adjust their lifestyles. . . . This is a great time to practice sexual monogamy."

The possible slowing down of the sexual revolution is good news. But there is painful irony in the fact that it took AIDS to accomplish what no amount of pulpit-pounding could do. People have a greater fear of disease than of God's judgment!

Such a low view of God in our supposedly Christian culture raises troubling questions for Christians. Is our view of God any higher? Where are we failing in presenting our message?

To be sure, we rant against immorality. But usually we lay the blame on the "permissive society" or on liberal legislation. And so we seek political solutions for our moral failures, rather than focusing on individual sin and warning of the consequences of incurring the wrath of a just and holy God.

And when we do preach about consequences, they aren't the *ultimate* judgments of a righteous God that Edwards preached about. No, the slickly marketed gospel shaped by the immediacy of television is a message of *immediate* consequences—the health, wealth, and business success that come to all who believe.

But if we preach only this gospel of temporal blessings, we are just like the pagan who alters his behavior because of immediate consequences rather than an ultimate fear of God. As British writer Harry Blamires has cautioned, "The real Christian Message must disturb. Sometimes it will disturb frighteningly, bringing as it does the sense of human weakness, sinfulness, and utterly abandoned dependence upon the Divine Mercy. . . . There must be Heaven in the Christian Message, and there must be Hell."

In a time such as this, be it an age of liberation or an age of restraint for the wrong reasons, we dare not water down the power of the real Christian message. People are dying to know it.

February 1986

Chapter Twenty-three

We Aren't the World

Ever since giving to the needy became chic in Hollywood, we've been treated to a billion-dollar bonanza of celebrities, benefit records, and sad-eyed Ethiopian children.

It was Band-Aid, the British concert to help starving children, that started the aid bandwagon rolling. Later came Live Aid, a marathon rock concert simulcast from London and Philadelphia.

Thereafter, since aid had become so fashionable, came Fashion Aid, a charity evening of *haute couture* in London, followed by a Hollywood benefit for Mexican earthquake victims. There was Farm Aid to focus on the plight of American farmers; and an AIDS benefit after Rock Hudson's death could only be thought of as AIDS aid.

Three more compassion extravaganzas occurred in May of 1986. Hands Across America linked a human chain from Los Angeles to New York to raise $100 million for domestic homelessness and hunger.

The Freedom Festival raised money for Vietnam veterans; and then there's my favorite, Sport Aid, which began with a runner leaving Ethiopia with a torch lighted from a refugee's campfire. He jogged to several European cities; then this tireless athlete flew to New York, torch in hand (I can't help wondering about those "no smoking" signs in airplane cabins); there he lighted a flame in Manhattan's United Nations Plaza, which signaled the start of simultaneous 10-kilometer runs around the world. The plan, said organizer Bob Geldof, mastermind of Live Aid, was to raise money to fight disease and hunger in Africa.

While we all agree that helping starving people is a good thing, this sudden aid frenzy does raise some practical questions.

First, in an industry where publicity is the ticket to success, one may be excused for wondering if celebrity participation in such well-heralded events is altogether altruistic. The *We Are the World* video, which has sold millions of copies, reminds us less of starving children than of the great humanitarianism of its showcase of rock idols. The goals may be worthy, but such slickly publicized charity can only bring to mind Biblical warnings against hiring trumpeters—or camera crews—to record one's good deeds.

We might put aside petty suspicions about motives if only we knew that those in need were being helped. But this raises a second question.

The *New Republic* reports that while USA for Africa, the organization behind Live Aid, appeals for contributions to help the starving, 55 percent of its money is instead waiting to be spent on "recovery and long-term development projects," something celebrity efforts may be ill-equipped to pull off.

Of the $92 million raised by Live Aid and Band Aid, *Newsweek* says only $7 million has gone to emergency relief. Another $6.5 million has been spent on trucks and ships to haul supplies; $20 million has been earmarked for projects like bridges in Chad. The rest sits in bank accounts somewhere.

Unfortunately, there is an apolitical illusion at work in much of the celebrity aid: the belief that government or establishment relief agencies are unnecessary, and all we need is Bruce Springsteen.

But even such noncontroversial goals as feeding the hungry can get bogged down in squabbles over how money and food should be distributed, or stymied at the Marxist-controlled ports of Ethiopia.

My third question concerns the amoral illusion in all this. Consider the highlight of the Live Aid concert, the steamy duet of rock stars Mick Jagger and Tina Turner.

Jagger's twenty-year career includes such dubious hits as "Sympathy for the Devil" and "Between the Sheets." Tina Turner, clad in black leather for the show, claims a number of prior lives, including a stint as the ancient Egyptian queen Hatshepsut. Their erotic tangle was surely as much an appeal to the lust of the crowd as to help the hungry.

There seems to be no sense of the incompatibility of noble ends and ignoble means. "A good tree cannot produce bad fruit, nor can a rotten tree produce good fruit," Jesus said flatly. There is a connection between charity, in the Biblical sense, and virtue. If promoting lust is wrong, then we must ask: Can the good of feeding the hungry be accomplished by evil?

Rock promoter Bill Graham says of celebrity aid, "It's an incredible power, knowing on any given day you can raise a million dollars." *Newsweek* observes, "Perhaps that is why Live Aid and Farm Aid were such oddly upbeat exercises in self-congratulation. An industry was celebrating its power. Far from challenging the complacency of an audience, such mega-events reinforce it. . . . Now, by watching a pop-music telethon and making a donation . . . fans can enjoy vicariously a sense of moral commitment."

All this leads to the most dangerous illusion of all: the impression that our celebrity idols discovered the hunger crisis and now, with their prime-time specials, have solved it.

Jagger, Turner, and company notwithstanding, feeding the hungry did not begin with Live Aid. Organizations like Catholic Relief Services, World Vision, the Salvation Army, and millions of local churches have long been feeding the hungry—without the razzle-dazzle so recently discovered by the rich and famous. Incentives have not been albums and the chance to see celebrities grind up against one another, but obedience to Christ's commands.

Bob Geldof recently announced that the Band-Aid campaign, its mission accomplished, will close down by December [1986]. "It's like a shooting star," he enthused.". . . [F]or once . . . absolutely good and absolutely incorruptible came and went and worked."

I wonder. Shooting stars don't feed hungry multitudes. The real tragedy of celebrity aid would be if the public believes that the need is over when the curtain comes down in Hollywood.

For the problem of hunger will still be with us—and so will Christ's command to feed the hungry.

June 1986

Chapter Twenty-four

"Men Without Chests"

The headline shocks came rapid-fire. There was hardly time to catch one's breath.

First came espionage charges against FBI agent Richard Miller. It was unthinkable—for the first time in the Bureau's proud history, an agent betrayed his trust.

Next was the bizarre tale of ex-Navy warrant officer John Walker, alleged ringleader of a spy ring that included his half-brother and young sailor son.

Days later, a covert operator for the CIA in Ghana, Sharon Scranage, was indicted on eighteen counts of espionage.

Then FBI agents arrested Colonel Wayne Gilespie, West Pointer and Vietnam veteran, for selling weapons to Iran.

The spate of cases sent tremors through Washington. Military brass promised a tightening of security, while Congress quickly voted on a capital punishment statute for spies.

The cases brought concern to the country as well. In VFW halls and hard-hat bars, in the churches and living rooms where folks still talk unashamedly about things like patriotism and duty, grief was mixed with anger. It seemed an epidemic was sweeping the very institutions most Americans revere as bastions of our values and liberties. Why?

Most commentators saw the scandals as simply individuals succumbing to age-old temptations. That is certainly plausible in a society that relentlessly pursues power, pleasure, and possessions; and such motives were apparent in each case.

John Walker played James Bond with gusto, dashing about in his plane, sailing his sloop in the company of glamorous women. His arrest crowned his fantasy as Walker crowed giddily, "I'm a celebrity!"

Greed might have snared Wayne Gilespie. The colonel, a twenty-nine-year veteran, was about to retire and enter the arms business. Other retired officers landed cushy jobs with defense contractors, so why shouldn't he get a head start? After all, only a fool doesn't take care of himself in our "look out for Number One" society.

Or take FBI agent Richard Miller. Father of seven, stuck in a paper-pushing post, and unable to meet his mortgage payments, he was no match for a modern Mata Hari, the sultry Russian woman who offered sex and money.

So it was with the CIA's Sharon Scranage, stationed at a lonely outpost in Ghana, swept off her feet by a businessman who just happened to be a cousin of Ghana's Marxist leader.

But payoffs and passion don't tell the whole story. These incidents are symptoms of an insidious cancer that has pervaded the values undergirding our public institutions.

This disease is not confined to the U.S., as recent scandals in Britain and West Germany reveal, but it is part of a general malaise erupting in the West wherever spiritual values are being sapped.

To understand it in the United States, one must return to the mid-sixties. Even as John Kennedy's "Ask not what your country can do for you, but what you can do for your country" rang in our ears, and Green Berets defended our "noble vision" in Southeast Asia, an undercurrent of protest churned. Campus flower children had another vision—easy sex, hard rock, hard drugs, and peace. Peace no matter what.

Then the "noble vision" bogged down in bloody rice paddies. With 55,000 of their buddies in body bags, the vets returned—not to ticker-tape parades, but to derision. And after Congress cut off aid to the nation they fought to save, the ex-soldiers witnessed the shame of panicked Americans dangling from the skids of overloaded helicopters and the U.S. flag burning in Saigon's streets.

The point here is not the wisdom or morality of American involvement in Vietnam. But this tragic war left millions disillusioned, and fueled growing discontent with our national purpose.

In the early seventies the media intensified the assault on authority. Then came Watergate—a breach of trust at the highest levels. Respect for institutions hit new lows. And what began as a campus movement became the age of the anti-hero. Disillusionment replaced the American dream.

In the light of this, should we really be shocked by today's spy cases? Consider Wayne Gilespie again. Ordered to fight, perhaps to die, in Vietnam, he returned to a nation that taunted its military for committing moral crimes against humanity. No wonder government lost its legitimacy, or that he might decide to rescue something from his career for himself. And since one war is no more moral than the next, why not sell a few arms to Iran?

Such reasoning is the inevitable result of our wholesale evisceration of values. Belief in "self-evident truths"—fixed standards by which right and wrong can be judged—has been replaced. Relativism, long lurking below the surface, emerged as the prevailing philosophy of the "me decade" of the seventies; it reigns in the yuppieism of the eighties.

We may still give lip service to traditional values, but in practice *right* is whatever is good for me. Emptied of meaning, words like duty and loyalty no longer have the moral force to restrain our passion for self-gratification.

C. S. Lewis did not live to see the America of the eighties. I doubt he's sorry he missed it. But he foresaw our situation today when he argued in 1943 that mere knowledge of right and wrong is powerless against man's appetites. Reason must rule the appetites by means of the "spirited element"—learned desires for the good, or "trained emotions," said Lewis. He likened reason to the head, the appetite to the stomach, and the spirited element—the essential connecting link—to the chest.

Aren't today's spy cases merely the consequence of a nation's loss of its spirited element? This is a sobering question for Christians, who have a special responsibility for a people's spirituality.

And if we are a nation of men without chests, so to speak, Lewis's description is all too apt: "We remove the organ and demand the function. We make men without chests and expect of them virtue and enterprise. We laugh at honor and are shocked to find traitors in our midst."

November 1985

Chapter Twenty-five

Jane Fonda's Farm Policies

I confess: I am not a morning person. Once upright, my greatest challenge is to focus in the mirror while shaving. To help me through the early fog I usually flip on the morning news shows, which serve as a conversational Muzak.

But one recent morning [1985] the background conversation suddenly caught my full attention. The familiar woolly-haired film critic was interviewing actress Liv Ullman. "There are no rules that can apply to [every]body and there [are] many kinds of truths," Ms. Ullman was saying. "The one which is easiest and best to live by is your own, the core within yourself." She concluded, "I never told my daughter that what I say is the truth."

I stared at the screen, shaving cream dripping from my face. Ms. Ullman may well be an accomplished actress, but does the fact that she is a screen celebrity also make her a philosopher for millions of morning TV viewers?

Soon after, I chanced upon a similar interview with Jerry Hall, rock star Mick Jagger's live-in girlfriend who has borne him two children. Phil Donahue managed such weighty questions as, "Was it a surprise when you got pregnant?," to which Hall replied, "Oh, yes, I was just lying there."

And here is Hall's cave-woman formula for keeping her man: "As long as the house is clean and organized and they are fed and have plenty of sex they'll never run away."

Even God gets his turn on the celebrity circuit.

Rita Jenrette, whose claim to notoriety was posing nude after her congressman husband stumbled into Abscam, is back in the news: she's found religion. While fervently hoping her conversion is genuine, one has to swallow hard over her suggestion that God is "neutral" about public nudity.

Or consider rock celebrity Prince, whose albums sell tens of millions. According to the media, he's "fervently religious"; his band joins hands in prayer before concerts, at which he combines overt sexuality with a song about Christ's crucifixion, or struts on the stage in his underwear claiming he's feeling fine "because the Lord is coming soon."

A concert last spring found nearly 13,000 young Prince fans chanting his lyrics like a liturgy: "I'm not a human. . . . I am your conscious [sic]. . . . I'm your messiah and you're the reason why."

Unfortunately, these are not isolated examples—for to command media attention these days, one need only be famous or near-famous. The reason for one's fame is irrelevant, except the more outrageous, the better.

So an interview about the value of life with Bernhard Goetz would score better Nielsen ratings than an interview with, say, an intellectual Nobel laureate; or, one on marriage and family with Elizabeth Taylor would top James Dobson. The goal is not to inform, but to entertain—if that's the word for the steady TV diet of banal puffery served up by these hollow figures called celebrities.

In his insightful new book *Intimate Strangers*, film critic Richard Schickel argues that television's dominance has made the cult of the celebrity inevitable.

By its nature TV requires "simplifying symbols"; thus it produces celebrities, which become the principal means to communicate ideas. Celebrities are the "chief agent[s] of moral change in America," concludes Schickel.

Consider just two consequences of this chilling phenomenon.

First, to affect public policy, images—often slickly crafted—are more important than reasoned argument. For example, President Reagan gallops out of the White House, larger than life, daring Congress to "make my day." His charisma makes him popular even when his policies aren't.

The other side combats with images of its own, as when actresses Jane Fonda, Jessica Lange, and Sissy Spacek appeared before a congressional committee to tearfully oppose Reagan's farm policies.

None is a farmer or an agricultural expert. But, in a fitting commentary on our times, they were called as witnesses because they had *played* farm women in recent films. "We knew when they came forward," gushed one political leader, "everyone would pay attention."

This leads to the second consequence—the ultimate, unconditional victory of style over substance. Societies have always looked up to philosophers, persons of learning and distinction, to provide wisdom and noble visions. But, as Schickel concludes, today it is the celebrity—famous or infamous—who "shape[s] minds and change[s] our traditional modes of apprehending and responding to the world."

Thus Liv Ullman gives us our philosophy, Jerry Hall our morality, Jane Fonda our farm policy, and, most frightening of all, rock star Prince gives the theology of the eighties.

With media glitz replacing informed discussion, the sublime becomes indistinguishable from the ridiculous. Thus is the populace morally desensitized.

It is the church, however, which is the soul of the nation; the church which must prick the national conscience. But I wonder if we can.

We too have been lured into the promised land of imagedom. Electronic communications demand simplified symbols—no less for great ideas than for selling books or soft drinks. So the gospel is packaged into slick "what God can do for you" sixty-second segments.

Said a Christian broadcaster interviewed on "60 Minutes": "The main thing is just to create an image. . . . You've got to present a product that's a little bit more appealing than the others." Mind you, he's speaking of the gospel.

And one has only to flip on Christian television or check our bookstores to confront the cult of the celebrity head-on. It's not so outrageously blatant as in the secular world, perhaps—we follow our own rules—but the idols are there in force.

Thus, what is bending the mind of America may be eroding its soul as well. And that is something to think about.

October 1985

Chapter Twenty-six

The Return of the Hero

D ecember is the time for pundits to analyze the year's news, identify trends, speculate about the future.

But though it probably won't rate in the year-end headline stories, I think a significant phenomenon may be developing. It's just beneath the surface, but carries profound implications for our national character. Once again Americans seem to be seeking authority figures and role models—heroes, if you will.

What makes this trend so dramatic is that it comes after two decades of systematic assault on traditional institutions and symbols of authority—an assault that began with the flower children of the sixties. Influenced by existential writers, they rejected their parents' traditional values, embracing instead a vision of easy sex, hard rock and "do your own thing"—at any price.

This campus protest soon invaded the mainstream of American culture. Journalism prospered by trashing politicians and institutions alike. Millions of Americans, disillusioned by Vietnam and Watergate, angrily questioned traditional authority structures.

Opinion polls reflected plummeting public respect for Congress, the military, and business. Patriotism was sneered at, and

America was painted, particularly by a carping Congress, as being on the wrong side of nearly every issue.

Popular literature mirrored narcissism, the hallmark of what writer Thomas Wolfe called the "me decade." Titles like *Looking Out for Number One*, *Winning by Intimidation*, and *How to Be Your Own Best Friend* dominated the best-seller lists; the hot magazine that evolved from that time was, fittingly, *Self*.

With self-absorption at its peak and authority debunked, there was no place for role models. Jane Fonda, an architect of the age, summed it up; when asked who her heroes were, she replied, "None."

But there are now [1985] signs that attitude may be changing. Look at 1985's best-sellers: *Iacocca* has broken records for hardback book sales. It's unadulterated Horatio Alger—an Italian immigrant's son scraps to the top, is canned by a tyrannical tycoon, only to rise again and rescue Chrysler.

Close on its heels is the biography of Chuck Yeager, the test pilot who broke the sound barrier. His story transports us from the impersonal age of computer-controlled missiles back to the glamorous days when daring aces cheated death to defeat our foes.

The same pattern has emerged in films. *Rambo* broke box-office records as Sylvester Stallone single-handedly refought and *won* the Vietnam war. And *Newsweek* picked Clint Eastwood, once berated for casually blowing away bad guys with his .44 Magnum, as the "new American icon."

Even politicians, after a long slump, seem to be gaining esteem. President Reagan has become a hero for millions, not so much for his policies as for his courage, first for recovering from an assassin's bullet, and then for facing down America's most dreaded killer, cancer.

A recent Roper poll shows public favor for institutions on the rise, with churches, the police, business, and industry leading the list.

It seems our respect for heroes and the authority structures they represent may be returning, Why?

For the most part, the reasons are healthy. Americans have seen the bankruptcy of the flower children's dream, which led not to the promised land but to a wilderness of despair. It seems too that Americans are realizing again that life cannot be lived without values, that authority structures are important, that we need legitimate goals and aspirations beyond self. These can be provided by role models, the heroes who inspire the rest of us and goad us on.

So where do we turn for such examples? This is where the ground gets mushy underfoot—and where the current trend may not be all good news after all.

For heroes, as those of us who have been around public figures can testify, have feet of clay. Having read *Iacocca*, I'm not sure I want my grandchildren emulating his ruthlessness. Chuck Yeager comes closer to being a genuine hero, I suppose, but he spoiled it for me when he attributed his victories to "luck, pure and simple." Politicians come and go; and much as we might wish otherwise, Rambo and Dirty Harry are only fictional characters.

So what I believe is a healthy development can also be a danger. The wrong heroes can lead us the wrong way. They breed supernationalism, arrogance, and eventual disillusionment.

But the new search for heroes offers those of us who are Christians a grand opportunity. For this month [December], we celebrate the birth of a true hero—one who came, not as a conqueror, but as a servant. Thus, like the people of His time, millions today fail to recognize Him.

This hero was born in a barnyard, the antithesis of our cultural expectations of power, stature, and influence. He gave His life to the poor and helpless, made the blind see, and ultimately died crucified between two thieves.

But His story did not end there.

A good way for us to celebrate Christmas is to point those who are hungering for heroes to the One who won't let them down, the one Hero who proved He is bigger than life by conquering death.

December 1985

Chapter Twenty-seven

Trouble in the School Yard

S tanding before a huge American flag, Barbara Walters looked sternly into the TV camera. "The alarm has sounded," she said. "The clock is ticking. But most of us are still asleep."

Nuclear threat? Acid rain? Imminent epidemic?

No. Walters was referring to the equally serious threat posed by the deterioration of American education. Test scores are plummeting. Most high-school students in her survey thought the Holocaust was "a Jewish holiday." Many couldn't locate the U.S. on a world map.

But Walters went further. The real crisis, she argued, is one of character. "Today's high-school seniors live in a world of misplaced values," she said. They have no sense of discipline. No goals. They care only for themselves. In short, they are "becoming a generation of undisciplined cultural barbarians."

We shouldn't be surprised. Modern education could not logically be expected to produce anything else.

Why? Because so-called "tolerant," "value-neutral" education, while purporting to teach no values, does in fact promote a value system of its own. And that value system is destructive to the moral restraints essential to character.

A friend recently sent me a videotape that illustrates this point. Titled "Sex, Drugs, and AIDS," it was shown in her son's high school and gives health information about how AIDS is transmitted and how it can be avoided. It even grudgingly mentions abstinence as a way to protect oneself.

But as the film ends, it becomes obvious that its agenda is not confined to AIDS information, but to teach that there's nothing wrong with homosexuality. A boy relates how he had been a gay-basher. But after discovering his own brother had AIDS, he realized that homosexuality was just another lifestyle option—one that he would not judge.

Many would defend "Sex, Drugs, and AIDS" as part of that grand American tradition known as Tolerance. Except that it is a subtle inversion of classic tolerance.

At one time *tolerance* meant that diversity could peacefully exist in our politically, morally, and ethnically diverse society. But our culture has become increasingly characterized by skepticism about absolute right and wrong; moral standards, and truth itself, are reduced to personal choices.

Tolerance is thus redefined as the freedom to choose from a smorgasbord of morally equivalent lifestyles—homosexuality, adultery, premarital promiscuity. Take your pick.

Allan Bloom calls this new tolerance "the virtue, the only virtue, which all primary education for more than fifty years has dedicated itself to inculcating." And this smorgasbord-style tolerance, itself a moral position, tramples on the sensibilities of any who hold to moral absolutes—particularly Christians.

"Sex, Drugs, and AIDS" is not an isolated example. A California sex-education curriculum titled *Intelligent Choice of Sexual Lifestyle* advises seventh-graders to set a "purely personal standard of sexual behavior." A sex-ed curriculum for *elementary* children specifies that they will "develop an understanding of homosexuality," view films, and act out homosexual roles. So ten-year-olds can get gold stars for homosexual role play.

The value-neutral trend is, of course, broader than just sexual issues. What's a concerned parent to do?

Parents could insist that public schools get rid of any reference to controversial moral matters—sanitizing education of anything that might conflict with instruction students receive at home. But this would reduce history, philosophy, and literature, even economics and English, to pallid gruel indeed.

Or parents could insist that when one moral position is presented in a public school, every other view must be taught as well. Equal time for opposing opinions. Though few teachers are equipped to dispassionately argue a variety of viewpoints well, this would at least provide some remedy to today's imbalance.

Or third—and perhaps best for those who can do it—Christian parents might abandon public schools altogether, teaching their children at home or enrolling them in Christian schools. But there is a real value in the diversity in public schools that reflects American society. It allows for instruction in real tolerance—civility, cooperation, and friendship with those who are different. In this environment the inevitable challenges to faith can result in a deepening of character.

Unfortunately, there's no simple answer. But one thing is certain. We can't look to the new administration or the media or educators themselves to truly address the crisis of values among the classroom barbarians. In the final analysis, the decisive battles will be fought in homes, in communities, before school boards and legislative committees. That means that you and I, parents and grandparents, must take up the standard.

When confronted with public schools that affirm moral positions contrary to our Christian ethic on the one hand, while self-righteously wielding the umbrella of "tolerance" with the other, we must do two things. First, we must continue to affirm Christian values in the home, equipping our children for the fray in the world outside.

And second, we must enter that fray ourselves, raising a ruckus, fighting the good fight, crying foul in the school yard. These are tests we cannot afford to fail.

April 1989

PART III

The Church

Chapter Twenty-eight

The God Who Is

I read an article some years ago that has haunted me ever since. A young man, formerly a skeptic toward Christianity, had "accepted Christ" and enrolled at a fine evangelical institution. Yet he emerged embracing not faith, but a renewed skepticism.

It's all a sham, he concluded. Sharing Christian faith is a matter of perfecting sales techniques and memorizing "five to fifteen verses of Scripture . . . strung together to form what the worker believes is an irrefutable presentation." Blanket a neighborhood with enough tracts, he writes, and you're sure to "win" a soul or two.

The critique is nothing new. Skeptics have long argued that Christianity is perpetuated solely by human techniques. Given human nature, if a certain target group is presented the evangelistic message, a predictable share will respond. *New . . . Improved . . . Salvation Lite*—on the market like soup or soap or shaving cream.

Admittedly some evangelists have lent credence to this notion. Revivalists in the last century—and some today—have argued that, if the gospel is presented faithfully, the results can be predicted with near-mathematical certainty.

But it is not up to evangelists to save souls. It is God who works in people's hearts—in often inexplicable ways—to quicken men and women dead in sin with new life in Christ.

I was given the clearest evidence last summer [1989] in Costa Rica. I wish the skeptics could have seen the colorful array of ministry workers from every corner of the globe—converted not by some evangelistic formula, but transformed by God Himself in the most amazing and original ways.

Consider Irina Ratushinskaya, the Soviet dissident and poet. When Irina was a girl, she was drilled in atheism, being told by her Communist teachers that there was no God. Irina had no reason to believe otherwise—no Sunday school, no Christian influences, no tracts or missionaries.

But, through the processes of a child's clean logic, God made Himself manifest to her. "There must be a God," she thought. "Otherwise they wouldn't tell us over and over that there is no God."

Much later, in her twenties, Irina finally got hold of a Bible—and saw that the God of the Scriptures was the same God she had met in her childhood. "Then I realized," she says today, "that I was a Christian."

Or Norma Todd, a woman from Australia who had known nothing but hate and violence all her life. When a policeman appeared at her door one day to tell her about Christ, she tried to beat him up. An alcoholic and a prostitute, Norma had no earthly reason to believe in a God of love.

Yet that God was inexorable. Norma couldn't resist His knock on the door of her heart; she yielded herself and was totally transformed.

And then there was Father Lawrence Jenco. I was captivated by Father Jenco's gripping tale about imprisonment as a hostage in Beirut, and not only the survival but the flourishing of his faith in the midst of terrible deprivation. And as I reflected on his story, I remembered another former hostage, Jerry Levin.

Jerry Levin called himself an atheist when he was first kidnapped by Moslem extremists in 1984. Perhaps he was simply an agnostic; God might exist, he thought, but if He did, He had no relevance in Jerry's life.

But as Jerry spent his days and nights blindfolded and chained to a radiator, he found that his thoughts turned increasingly to the One whose existence he doubted. He figured he would either go crazy or talk to God. But feeling that if even the most minute part of him doubted the existence of God he would be just talking to himself, he knew he had to *believe.*

"Ten days after my meditating began," Jerry says, "I approached and then crossed a kind of spiritual Rubicon, a diminishing point in time, a shrinking thousandth, then millionth of a second on one side of which I did not believe and then on the other side I did."

Thus Jerry Levin came to faith in God, and later to faith in Jesus—without a Bible, an evangelist, an invitation, or a tract. The Holy Spirit called him to the Godhead through Christ.

As I heard the incredibly varied testimonies from my co-laborers in ministry from sixty countries, I was overwhelmed by the irrefutable evidence of God's grace and the inexorability of His call in each of our lives.

Sometimes the Holy Spirit speaks in a still, small voice in a Beirut prison cell, or in the reflections of a small Russian girl reared in official atheism. Some come to faith through evangelistic crusades; others through the witness of the most unlikely person they could have imagined.

No one could witness the Costa Rica convocation and believe that Christianity is a human invention, that Christians are stamped out cookie-cutter style. No, the breezes of the Holy Spirit blow where He chooses; we see the movement in human lives and the evidence that He has been there.

Would that the skeptics could see in us not sales pitches and tract tossing, but the reflection of this God who is.

March 1990

Chapter Twenty-nine

An Antidote to Christian-Bashing

The radio host nodded as the "on the air" sign flashed and the seventy-fifth interview of my book tour began. Outside the studio's floor-to-ceiling windows the gleaming clusters of Dallas's glass skyscrapers competed for attention, monuments of a proud and confident city.

This was one of Dallas's most popular interview shows, and a great opportunity. I was primed to talk about the loss of spiritual values in American life and the need for Christian involvement in the public arena.

"We have with us Chuck Colson, author of *Kingdoms in Conflict*," the interviewer began. "But first," he chuckled, "let's hear what 'God's little goofballs' have for us today." He flipped a switch and a prerecorded phone message from Jim and Tammy Bakker filled the airwaves. In the control room I could see sound technicians laughing and rolling their eyes. The message ended—mercifully— and my host turned toward me. "And now," he smiled, "let's hear what Mr. Colson has to say."

His introduction wasn't the shock it might have been. Most of my tour interviews had started with questions about Jim and

Tammy or other well-publicized religious excesses. Christian-bashing is in high fashion these days, and I was at first defensive. But soon I got angry, as I did this day.

"There have been some dreadful mistakes," I said, "but why judge all Christians by the few who abuse their position? There are 350,000 churches across America where people's spiritual needs are being met. Thousands of missionaries are living in conditions you or I couldn't. Thousands of volunteers are working in the prisons, soup kitchens, and rescue missions. That's the church in action!" I was almost shouting into the microphone.

The interviewer smiled. Reason, after all, is no match for ridicule.

After finally digging out of the Bakker rubble, I was able to get into my material: the Kingdom of God and how its citizens transform the kingdoms of man by living in obedience to Christ. But even as I spoke, I wondered if my words could even begin to alter the stereotypes they were up against. As critic Neil Postman has written in his insightful book *Amusing Ourselves to Death*, we are fast moving from a word-oriented society to one that is image-oriented.

Values are no longer formed by rational discourse; in fact, we have nearly discarded the vocabulary necessary to do so. Instead, an image is transmitted—the grinning faces or gushing voices of Jim and Tammy, for example—and the caricatured message is complete. Mascara and money manipulation become emblems for the church at large—and nothing more need be said.

By the time I had finished in that Dallas studio, the book tour had taken its toll. I'd squared off against scoffers, skeptics, and secularists until I was hoarse. But to what avail? Could anything really change the image of Christianity so entrenched in the public consciousness?

As it happened, only a few days after my dismaying encounter in Dallas I was scheduled to break ground for a prison chapel in Delaware and attend a Prison Fellowship dedication service.

Georgetown, Delaware, is a small town surrounded by chicken farms and cornfields. The closest thing to a skyscraper there is a grain-storage silo.

The town's dignitaries and Delaware's lieutenant governor were waiting inside the gates of the state prison when I arrived for the ground-breaking. The chaplain, an open-faced Baptist named Larry Lilly, introduced each of us for brief remarks. The most eloquent came from Jim, a heavy-set inmate serving life without parole. He told how volunteers had ministered to him, what Jesus had come to mean to him, how he and his brothers were free, even in prison. Jim struggled to control his emotions as he thanked the local churches for supporting the project.

The 275-seat chapel, which is to be built by volunteers and inmates with local funds, will stand in the center of the prison yard, surrounded by drab cellblocks and razor wire. As we concluded the ground-breaking by turning over shovelfuls of black soil, I thought of the miracle before us: a church planted in the middle of humanity's hell on earth.

We adjourned to Grace United Methodist Church, where supper would be served before the evening service. It was to be a celebration concluding Prison Fellowship's Community Service Project, a program in which five prisoners, furloughed to the care of Christian host families, had worked for two weeks restoring a senior citizens' center and the home of an elderly retired couple.

Mennonite farm families, the women's hair tucked neatly into white net caps, the men wearing suspenders over their plaid wool shirts, served steaming platters of roast turkey, bowls of crisp home-grown vegetables, hot baked buns, and homemade pumpkin ice cream. I'd been to White House state dinners that could not top this feast.

The sanctuary soon grew warm as we all crowded into the old oak pews for the evening service. In the last row sat Delaware's commissioner of corrections, wide-eyed as his prisoners spoke movingly about their experience. Men who wouldn't dare cry in prison choked up as they described how much it had meant to live with Christian families, to accomplish something useful for society, and to grow in their faith.

As the service closed, the chaplain asked each of the host

families to stand at the altar with "their" inmate. As they lined up before the congregation, one little blonde girl—maybe six or seven—took the hand of the prisoner who had lived in her home, looking up into his eyes throughout the concluding prayer. His eyes were misty. So were mine.

I needed to be in Georgetown for that simple Sunday service; it put my book tour experiences into perspective. Yes, there is a wide gulf between Dallas and Delaware, between the image and the reality of Christianity. It is a gulf so wide, in fact, that maybe it can't be closed. But does that really matter so much after all? The image may reign, but beyond the caricatures of television and radio stations, the reality lives on.

March 1988

Chapter Thirty

A Message for All Seasons

Several years ago a newly appointed Anglican bishop, David Jenkins, created a ruckus in England when he questioned the virgin birth of Christ.

Jenkins evidently enjoyed the furor; in a second pronouncement he dismissed Christ's resurrection as a "conjuring trick with bones." That colorful phrase was widely reported by an amused secular press.

A few days later a dramatic event turned the story into front page news: Yorkminster, the beautiful cathedral belonging to the diocese of Jenkins's archbishop, was struck by a mysterious bolt of lightning that knocked its thirteenth-century oak ceiling beams to the flagstone floor.

A flood of articles ensued, most provocatively headlined, "Coincidence or the Wrath of God?" But the story soon faded. Just as well, I thought. It was, after all, merely the prattle of a heretical bishop, sensationalized by the media.

(It was not all that startling either, considering the views of Jenkins's colleagues: a poll had just revealed that of the thirty-one

Anglican bishops in England, nineteen said that to be a Christian one need only believe that Jesus was God's supreme moral agent. Only eleven bishops said that one must accept Jesus as fully God and fully man!)

But Jenkins's blasphemous statement did not just blow over, as I discovered during a recent visit [written in 1986] to the Near East. In Sri Lanka, when I asked Desmond Goonasekera, an Anglican rector and chairman of Lanka Prison Fellowship, about the growth of the Christian church in his country, he shook his head. "We're losing badly to the Moslems," he said. "It all began with the Jenkins business."

He explained that aggressive Moslems were visiting Christian communities, using Bishop Jenkins's quote as authoritative proof that Christians need no longer believe in Christ's resurrection. Since Moslems and Christians now see Jesus as merely a prophet, they argued, why not worship together in the mosque? "They are killing us with our bishop's own words," Desmond concluded.

What I had dismissed as one man's heresy had become a stumbling-block to Christian faith halfway around the world—a sobering reminder of the grave consequences of trifling with the truth.

During the same trip, I also saw the other side of the coin: the convicting power of the uncompromising truth of the gospel. In India, wherever I presented my testimony, the predominantly Hindu crowds would nod and smile in approval. At first I was startled: how could they be so amenable to what Christ had done in my life? But as a Delhi pastor reminded me, Hindus believe all roads lead to God. If Jesus was my guru, fine. They all had their gurus too.

I realized, then, that personal testimony often is not enough, particularly in Eastern cultures. Though we Western evangelicals often use personal testimony as the primary formula for our evangelism, we must never forget that Christianity rests upon the historic truth of Christ's rising from the dead. Whenever I presented the Resurrection and the evidence that proves it, people's expressions changed. They listened intently. Such a message demands a choice; it reduces all other religions to abstract philosophies.

For example, at a luncheon meeting in Bombay, after I had presented the case for the Resurrection, a large, round-faced man introduced himself as the editor of the *Islamic Times*. Smiling broadly and thrusting out his hand, he told me that as a Moslem he believed the same things I did.

I hesitated. This man seemed so friendly, and I was a guest in his country; perhaps I shouldn't disturb our rapport. But then, almost irresistibly, the words rushed out: "But we don't believe the same thing, for I believe that Jesus was bodily raised from the dead."

The man's grin vanished. "I know," he said soberly, "and you've made a very strong case. I must think about it." With that, he turned and walked away. I learned later that he immediately visited a group of Christian businessmen, saying that he had to "examine the evidence."

I returned from Sri Lanka and India with a renewed appreciation of why the great evangelist, Paul, staked the entire case for Christianity on the Resurrection—and the grave consequences of stripping this central truth from the gospel.

Happily, evangelicals do not flatly deny the Resurrection as did Bishop Jenkins. But I wonder if we don't do similar damage when, in our efforts to attract the multitudes, we preach primarily of what God will do for us—whether it be personal peace, the healing of broken relationships, or the health-and-wealth gospel so commonly hawked on Christian radio and TV.

We must not dilute the gospel by ignoring the Cross—or from the seeds of our evangelism will sprout followers attracted to Christianity for what it will give them, rather than out of love and service for a risen Lord. We follow Christ not because of His blessings, but because He is truth.

If indeed Jesus was bodily raised (and He was!), that is the most important fact of human history. It establishes the Deity of Christ, validates what He taught, and demonstrates that He was and is the only true God. It not only undermines every other religious claim, but it crosses all ethnic, religious, and cultural barriers.

The Resurrection is not, then, just an event we celebrate at Easter, but rather the heart of Christian evangelism—the message for all seasons to a needy world.

March 1986

Chapter Thirty-one

The Pedestal Complex

I recently suffered through a depressing but necessary experience—reading Charles Shepard's *Forgiven*, the painfully detailed
account of the rise and fall of Jim Bakker.

It was depressing because the story contains all the elements of
classic Greek tragedy: a leading character trapped in his own web
of deceit. Only this isn't ancient literature, it's real life. And the
tragedy has wrought incalculable harm upon the cause of Christ.

Studying the book was necessary, however, because of its
sobering lessons for the thousands of us in Christian service. As I
read, I was reminded how vulnerable we all are. Let no one be self-
righteous: The terrifying truth is that what happened to Bakker
could happen to any of us.

But as I labored through the pages of *Forgiven*, another lesson
came home to me, one that applies to the evangelical movement as
a whole: In a sense we created Jim Bakker, or at least the lethal environment in which he fell. This is not to excuse his misdeeds, but the
lesson is plain. Jim Bakker's demise was the nearly inescapable consequence of a popular idolatry: celebrity worship.

Raised in a modest Muskegon, Michigan, neighborhood, a

poor student with a self-confessed inferiority complex, Bakker managed only three semesters of Bible college before launching out on a small-town revival circuit. When Jim was twenty-five, his and Tammy's puppet show for kids hit the big time on then-fledgling Christian television.

Fame came fast. Adoring crowds heaped mountains of money on the "house" that Jim built, gorgeous buildings full of high-tech studios. Jet-setters, Jim and Tammy cruised Palm Springs in leather-lined limousines, and were even courted by presidential candidates.

Such instant fame has destroyed countless celebrities. Most of us are not as immune to pride as Mother Teresa.

Celebrity worship has become so pervasive that, as Richard Schickel writes in *Intimate Strangers*, it substitutes "for a sense of organization, purpose, and stability in our society." This is understandable perhaps in the values vacuum of secular America; but the baffling part is that Christians have fallen into the same trap.

We evangelicals mindlessly elevate our own superstars: honey-tongued TV preachers, baby-faced World Series heroes, converted rock stars, and yes, a former White House aide who supposedly would have run over his own grandmother.

We worship fame for fame's sake. So what if the celebrity is long on outward looks and short on inward substance? Theological depth, spiritual maturity, and even integrity matter less than worldly fame.

There are at least two possible explanations for this very non-Biblical attitude.

One is that ordinary citizens who may feel insignificant in this super-hyped media age can experience power and privilege vicariously through the celebrity. Why else do widows living on Social Security send their $10 or $20 checks to televangelists who wear Rolex watches and live in ministry-provided palatial estates? Somehow these supporters must be living out the fantasy of the Christian high life right along with the celebrity, a phenomenon Schickel describes at length in his book.

There is a second explanation: The celebrity affirms our faith.

"If God could convert him," I remember people saying about me, "he can convert anyone." This leads to a tendency to paint the convert's past more sinful and his present more saintly than either deserves. I know.

Shortly after my release from prison I was waiting to give my testimony to a packed auditorium of students. A former White House colleague, on hand to introduce me, leaned over and whispered to the emcee, "I'm going to tell the audience what a great guy Chuck was before." The emcee turned ashen. "No, no," he stammered, "you'll ruin the whole thing."

But the danger of celebrityism in the Christian world is not just that we puff up mere mortals with pride, put them on pedestals, throw our coins at them, and then shake our heads disgustedly when they fall. No, there is a less obvious but even more deadly effect of Christian idol-worship: Celebrityism lets individual believers off the hook.

It's tragic that the illusions of our culture have us believing that only big names or big organizations can accomplish anything. And so we send our checks off to worldwide Christian ministries and settle back in the easy chair. We serve God by remote control.

In truth, the most important work of the gospel is done directly by citizens living out their Biblical responsibility in their everyday circumstances. This is one reason I look forward to visiting Third World countries. In most there are no evangelical superstars, no big organizations, and so those "poor" Christians simply go out and do the gospel themselves.

In Peru, for example, during last year's [1989] financial crisis the government cut funds for prisons, threatening food supplies for 7,000 inmates at the infamous Luringancho prison. Volunteers went door to door, filling trucks with canned goods, home-cooked stews, or whatever they could gather. When those trucks rolled through Luringancho's imposing gates, they were greeted by swarms of inmates. As the volunteers busily served the food, the inmates spontaneously broke out in hymns of praise.

These Christians had to trust solely in God to work through

their hands. I was confronted with a similar story in Madagascar where I found that the diligent efforts of one man kept alive several hundred inmates. I was so moved I asked if there was anything I could do to help, expecting him to say, "Send money." "Oh no," came his astonishing reply, "our God is sufficient for all things."

Those simple words and solid examples are a sobering message for today's evangelicals: We must forsake the worship of Christian megamen—which, as the Bakker tragedy showed us, spells doom—and get on with our duty to do the gospel. Our faith belongs not in corruptible media icons, but in our God who is sufficient for all things.

February 1990

Chapter Thirty-two

Giving God the Pink Slip

A group of scholars met recently to determine the authenticity of Christ's Gospel statements. They distributed among themselves colored slips of paper; a red slip meant the particular statement under consideration was "authentic," pink for "probably authentic," gray for "probably not authentic," and black for "not authentic." One by one Jesus' statements were considered; debate concluded with the solemn raising of the colored cards.

The Beatitudes and the Sermon on the Mount took a beating in the balloting. "Blessed are the peacemakers" was swiftly voted down. "Blessed are the meek" got only six timid red and pink votes out of thirty cast.

In the final count, only three of twelve assorted blessings and woes from Matthew and Luke were deemed authentic.

Unfortunately, this is not the isolated instance of theological tomfoolery that it first appears to be. Rather, it is symptomatic of serious efforts these days by serious-minded people to trivialize truth. Take, for example, the recent case of Father Charles Curran, professor of theology at Washington, D.C.'s Catholic

University, who is viewed as one of the nation's most influential theologians.

One small problem: Father Curran disagrees with just about every tenet of Roman Catholic (and traditional Christian) teaching on biomedical and sexual issues. He argues that divorce should be allowed, that abortion can be justified in the first two to three weeks after conception, that homosexuality can be "objectively morally acceptable," and that premarital sexual relations can occasionally be permitted on the basis of a "theology of compromise."

It's easy to see why Father Curran has long been viewed with suspicion by the Vatican. Finally, Rome forbade Curran to expound his views in the name of the church.

Curran immediately called a press conference. "[It's] my church as much as anyone else's . . . my church is a big church. . . . My God is a big God; yes She is."

The delighted media portrayed this as a modern David versus an antiquated Goliath: Curran was the heroic defender of academic freedom against a mammoth, repressive church. One columnist accused the church of "digging itself into irrelevancy" by its "backward-looking orthodoxy" and noted, "Polls show most Catholics agree with Curran." Another commented, "Such sanctification of the past, in the name of either God or mammon, cripples mankind's ability to face today's dilemmas."

The few writers who defended the church generally did so on the basis of the "McDonald's argument": You can't work for McDonald's and sell Wendy's burgers.

But the public debate has only touched surface issues. Like the New Testament balloting, the Curran controversy raises deeper questions about the nature of the church, as well as the very truth the church claims to uphold.

First, does a church have the right to set and enforce its own rules? Not if it is the democracy Curran and his supporters seem to suggest. Theology, one gathers, can be voted in or out according to public opinion polls.

But a church run by the whims of transient majorities is a sorry sight. Joseph Sobran comments, "It can be exalting to belong to a church that is five hundred years behind the times and sublimely indifferent to fashion; it is mortifying to belong to a church that is five minutes behind the times, huffing and puffing to catch up."

The church (not just Catholic or Protestant, but the universal church) is not a democracy. It can never be subject to majority rule. Its authority comes not from the consent of the governed, but from Christ its Head, who rules through Scripture and the Holy Spirit.

Father Curran's challenge raises a second, even more fundamental question: What is the nature of truth itself?

Curran claims that "The word and work of Jesus must always be made present and meaningful in the contemporary historical and cultural circumstances." Shifting sexual practices require the theologian, according to Curran, "to look at church teachings in light of these changes." Thus he views it as his responsibility "to push and probe" since "that is the only way change happens, even though the process is sometimes painful."

The Curran controversy is symptomatic of a relativism in which moral truths change with the regularity of interest rates: If society merely seeks the greatest good for the greatest number, why not let the greatest number define their own good? If a rule is most often broken, change it.

The historic Christian view, however, is that such considerations as "Is it difficult?" and "What do most people believe?" are irrelevant to determining belief. There is only one question: "Is it true?"

Such truth is based on belief in an unchanging, holy God whose will is revealed in Scripture. Our choice is to rebel or obey. We are not, in Norman Podhoretz's words, "free to decide that error is truth and sin is virtue."

Father Curran may be a folk hero today, but I think G. K. Chesterton's description may be more accurate: "We often read nowadays of the valor or audacity with which some rebel attacks a hoary tyranny or an antiquated superstition. There is not really any courage at all in attacking hoary or antiquated things, any more than in offering to fight one's grandmother. The really courageous man is he who defies tyrannies young as the morning and superstitions fresh as the first flowers."

November 1986

Chapter Thirty-three

Seamless Garment or Straitjacket?

This has been a particularly poor century for being human. Already more than 100 million men, women, and children have suffered violent death as a result of war, genocide, forced collectivization, inhuman prison conditions, and state-induced famine. Millions more have died as a result of "private" actions—decisions to abort unborn children, to withhold treatment from handicapped newborns, to hasten the death of elderly parents.

Traditional restraints on inhumanity seem to be crumbling—in the courts, the laboratory, the operating room, the legislature. The very idea of an essential dignity to human life seems but a quaint anachronism, no match for ideology or convenience or progress.

But when it comes to human life, Christians can't concede any ground. We are called to take up the cause of the weak, the helpless, the defenseless. It is our duty—that which, in large part, defines us as citizens of the Kingdom of God. Christians, in short, must be unequivocally, resolutely, and unapologetically pro-life.

Few Christians would have trouble accepting that label. But the real issue is more problematic; how one defines the term makes all the difference in one's focus and agenda. If, for example, "pro-life" means respect for both life and the natural process that creates it, one would naturally oppose contraception. If one defines it to include some minimum level of income, one would be led to support welfare programs for the poor.

What concerns me is that one popular definition of "pro-life," in spite of the best intentions of those who espouse it, is fundamentally flawed, even dangerous.

In a February 1988 speech, Joseph Cardinal Bernardin of Chicago attacked those who call themselves pro-life because of their stand against abortion, but who don't support what he calls a "consistent ethic of life." "We must refute decisively," he argued, "claims that we are a 'one issue' constituency."

What are the neglected pro-life issues according to Bernardin? Racial tension, homelessness, Reagan Administration economic policies, and, above all, nuclear deterrence. "We are committed to reversing the arms race and reversing *Roe v. Wade*," he concluded.

Bernardin has labeled his argument "the seamless garment"—the idea that to be consistently pro-life one must oppose both abortion and nuclear deterrence, euthanasia, and the economic exploitation inherent to industrial capitalism—anything, in short, that its proponents believe threatens human life and dignity.

A growing number of evangelicals, particularly on the "evangelical Left," echo this approach. After all, on the surface it seems plausible enough, offering a comprehensive alternative to a culture whose respect for life has become alarmingly selective. And it successfully avoids the charge of hypocritical attention to one life issue at the expense of others.

But herein lies the danger: This sweeping definition of the seamless garment leads some, logically indeed, to conclude that deterrence is immoral, and a few even to argue for unilateral nuclear disarmament. Even those who don't go that far convey the impression, by picking up the rhetoric, that no Christian could support deterrence.

I have always taken the term "pro-life" to mean that all human life, unborn or elderly, mentally or physically handicapped, should be given the same high value. But the effect of radical applications of the seamless garment is to push this definition much further. In spite of a range of nuance and sophistication among its advocates, some transform respect for life into veneration of life. Biological life becomes the principal, overriding human value. Anything that threatens it must be resisted. Thus, we have the opposition to taking life in the abortuary or on the battlefield.

The question then naturally arises: What price are we prepared to pay to preserve biological life? If we are willing to protect life at any cost, then the price we pay will be high. If the preservation of life is worth any sacrifice, any concession, any compromise, then the result, in a hostile world, can only be slavery.

Some things, such as justice and freedom, must be more important than life if life is to be worth anything at all. If we lack the moral resolve to die, and even to kill, so as to preserve these principles against those who assault them, then we will end up both betraying our principles and losing our lives.

The painful fact is that Christians are not exempt from agonizing conflicts of conscience. Taking a life or even many lives may be justified to prevent a far greater evil. It is for this very reason, I believe, that one cannot label nuclear deterrence immoral; in a world of brutal ideologies and vicious tyrannies, where justice and liberty are scarce and growing scarcer, the existence of nuclear weapons can be, as has been demonstrated for forty years, a powerful restraint on an intolerable evil.

C. S. Lewis wrote, ". . . it is part of our spiritual law never to put survival first: not even the survival of our species. We must resolutely train ourselves to feel that the survival of Man on this Earth, much more of our own nation or culture or class, is not worth having unless it can be had by honorable and merciful means."

That may sound fatalistic, but Lewis thought it was quite the opposite. "The sacrifice is not so great as it seems. Nothing is more likely to destroy a species or a nation than a determination to survive at all costs. Those who care for something else more than civilization are the only people by whom civilization is at all likely to be preserved."

In this light, the distinction between respect for life and veneration of life is as wide as the chasm between civilization and barbarism. Paradoxically, venerating life is life-negating, not life-affirming. It holds every other human value hostage and then one by one executes them.

We are called to be pro-life. But when we worship biological life we betray our principles and our lives. The only truly seamless garment, in the end, is a straitjacket.

November 1988

Chapter Thirty-four

Whatever Happened to Right and Wrong?

During a visit to an Australian prison in November 1986, I met a young man due to be released the next week. "Are you going to stay out?" I asked.

He smiled, rolled his eyes, and replied. "Well, it all depends on how they treat me out there."

Surprised, I asked who "they" were.

"You know, mate, the people on the outside. I mean, whether they take care of me or not—a job and a place to stay and all that sort of thing."

"Do you mean that you're letting other people decide for you what happens in your life?" I asked. "That you're not man enough to make your own decisions about what you're doing to do?"

The prisoner bristled; then he relaxed and shrugged. "Well, how am I supposed to make it on the outside if somebody doesn't help me?"

I explained that there are plenty of Christians to help; that's what Prison Fellowship does. "But," I continued, "you have to want to do it on your own and realize that what happens to you is the result of your own decisions, not somebody else's."

Clearly, such thoughts had never crossed his mind.

Sadly, I've seen this same attitude in every prison I've visited. Many prisoners simply don't believe they are responsible for their actions. For years experts have told them that crime results from poverty, from discrimination, from unemployment. So, the reasoning goes, society, not the individual, is at fault and must be changed.

This "enlightened" view has perpetuated a delusion that makes rehabilitation impossible. Prisoners, like everyone else, must first realize that they are responsible for their own behavior. Before they can change, they must understand that they need to change.

Because of this, the counseling of prisoners demands compassionate confrontation, including the delineation of right from wrong that will help excavate moral sensibilities rather than bury them.

The church is the only institution that can make those distinctions according to the truth of God's Word. But Christians are deeply divided over this very issue of the purpose and nature of counseling.

On one side people are convinced that counselors should never confront but only help counselees find truth in their own way and time. One Christian counselor writes, "The counselor should listen, show no authority, give no advice, not argue, talk only to aid or relieve or praise or guide and to clarify his problem." This stance is consistent with that of a secular psychologist who warns, "Advice-giving is not an adequate counseling function because it violates the autonomy of personality."

I recently received a letter from a friend whose church had been funding a Christian counseling center. When he discovered the center was recommending abortions, he was outraged and wrote to a well-known Christian psychologist for advice. In return he received a letter that shocked him.

"Counseling is nonspecific in terms of outcome," it said. This professional did not think that counselors should try to persuade counselees to take a particular course of action. Rather, they should help people work through their feelings and come to their own resolutions.

When he relayed his concern to me, my friend's questions became my own. Is it responsible for a Christian to be "nonspecific" in terms of outcome when it comes to abortions—or homicide, suicide, or infidelity? Should we not confront individuals with their own responsibility? As former Denver Seminary president Vernon Grounds comments, "No *Christian* therapist can sidestep a plain disclosure of his own ethical stance if a counseling relationship is to be open and authentic."

At the other end of the spectrum are Christians who believe counseling should always be both Scriptural and confrontational. All nonorganic mental problems result from sin, they say. People feel mental distress because they rely on feelings and because their lives revolve around themselves.

Of course, many Christians hold views that lie between these two poles. While I profess no expertise in counseling or psychology, I do have deep convictions based on eleven years of experience dealing with prisoners. I realize that some mental disorders are not the result of one's own immediate sin—drug-induced brain damage can impair people's ability to follow through on their own decisions; experiences like child abuse can deeply scar a person for life. Yet the fact remains that the overwhelming disorder of our time is moral.

This is the key to criminal behavior, the key to all human behavior: We are sinners, and we *choose* good or evil. A multitude of other factors—our skin color and nationality, the quality of our homes and neighborhoods, our parents and friends—influence what we do and become. But in the end, we are responsible for what we do.

In their book *The Criminal Personality*, Stanton Samenow and Samuel Yochelson describe their careful study of 250 habitual criminals. When they began, Samenow and Yochelson held the conventional view that criminals were victims of abuse and deprivation. They were looking for the social, psychological, or economic factors that could be said to "cause" crime.

To their surprise, they couldn't find any. They did find one thing that habitual lawbreakers had in common: given a choice, they chose to break the law.

While Christians must show compassion, sensitivity, and a willingness to meet people at their point of need, we must also unflinchingly stand for absolute standards put forth by a holy God. For it is the church's duty to call men and women to identify right and wrong and to accept responsibility for their behavior. Such a call to accountability may shock some prisoners and ex-prisoners with whom we work, as my statement shocked the Australian inmate—but this is the only way we can best serve those who come to us for help.

May 1987

Chapter Thirty-five

My Cancer and the Good-Health Gospel

Coming out of the anesthesia, I first saw the smiling faces of my wife, Patty, and daughter, Emily. "Did they get it all?" I asked. Patty gripped my hand. "Yes."

"Was it malignant?" I asked.

Emily nodded. "Yes, Daddy—it was cancer. But they got it all, and you're going to be okay."

Cancer.

I had always wondered, in secret fear, what it would be like to be told I had cancer. I thought I would be shattered. But I had prayed for the grace to withstand whatever the doctors found. And, as many have discovered before me, I saw in the confrontation with fear and suffering that there is nothing for which God does not pour out His grace abundantly. I felt total peace—and great thankfulness that a merciful God had brought me to that recovery room.

My stomach problems began in November 1986 during a ministry trip to the Philippines. I flew home. My doctor told me that I was badly rundown, that I had a bleeding ulcer, and to stay away from airports for a while. With rest and proper diet, the problem was soon cured.

Just when my stomach seemed fine, I talked with a dear Christian brother, Dr. Joe Bailey of Austin, Texas. Joe urged me, as my own internist had already done, to have a gastroscopy. The idea of inhaling a tube so doctors could view the scenery inside my stomach was not particularly inviting. Besides, the ulcer had already healed. But Joe kept insisting.

So I submitted to the horrors of the gastroscope. The doctor told me, as I had expected, that the ulcer was gone. Then came the unexpected: he had discovered a tumor in my stomach lining.

After weeks of additional tests, experts concluded the growth was benign. There was no reason to hurry to have it removed. Once again Joe Bailey called. "Chuck," he said in his Texas drawl, "get that thing out, and get it out as quick as you can."

"I can't," I told Joe. "I'm writing a new book. I have ministry commitments, speaking obligations." But Joe would not be moved. And since by then I suspected that God was speaking through him, I scheduled the operation for early January.

To everyone's surprise, the tumor was a low-grade malignancy. Because it was caught early, however, doctors have assured me my prognosis is excellent. If it had gone undetected, the outcome could have been far different. The previous fall's nagging ulcer served as a warning by which God got my attention—and then he used Joe Bailey's stubborn concern to get me into the hospital.

God's grace provided not only peace and protection, but new purpose. I had, as some friends know, begun to burn out from too many writing, speaking, and ministry commitments.

But as I lay in my hospital bed, I thought through my real priorities. Had I unconsciously boarded the evangelical treadmill? Trying to do all those worthy things that everybody wanted me to do, had I become beholden to a tyrannical schedule rather than to God's will? Several weeks tied to hospital tubes is a good time to reflect on the larger perspective of God's design in our lives.

My suffering provided some fresh insights as well into the health-and-wealth gospel. If God really delivers His people from all pain and illness, as is so often claimed, why was I so sick? Had my faith become weak? Had I fallen from favor?

No. I had always recognized such teaching as false theology. But after four weeks in a maximum-care unit, I came to see it as something else: a presumptuous stumbling-block to real evangelism.

During my nightly walks through the hospital corridors dragging an IV pole behind me, I often met an Indian man whose two-year-old son had had two failed kidney transplants, a brain aneurysm, and was now blind for life.

When the father, a Hindu, discovered I was a Christian, he asked if God would heal his son if he, too, was born again. He said he had heard things like that on television.

As I listened, I realized how arrogant health-and-wealth religion sounds to suffering families: Christians can all be spared suffering, but little Hindu children go blind. One couldn't blame a Hindu or Muslim or agnostic for resenting, even hating, such a God.

I told my Hindu friend about Jesus. Yes, He may miraculously intervene in our lives. But we come to God not because of what He may do to spare us suffering, but because Christ is Truth. What He does promise us is much more—the forgiveness of sin and eternal life. I left the hospital with my friend studying Christian literature, the Bible, and my own account in *Born Again*. If he becomes a Christian, it won't be on false pretenses.

I thought often in the hospital of the words of Florida pastor Steve Brown. Steve says that every time a non-Christian gets cancer, God allows a Christian to get cancer as well—so the world can see the difference. I prayed I might be so filled with God's grace that the world might see the difference.

Steve's words represent a powerful truth. God does not witness to the world by taking His people out of suffering, but rather by demonstrating His grace through them in the midst of pain.

He allows such weakness to reveal his strength in adversity. His own Son experienced brokenness—and died—that we might be freed from the power of death. But we are promised no freedom from suffering until we are beyond the grave.

Thus, I can only believe that God allowed my cancer for a purpose—just as He allows far more horrific and deadly cancers in fellow Christians every day. We don't begin to know all the reasons why. But we do know that our suffering and weakness can be an opportunity to witness to the world the amazing grace of God at work through us.

April 1987

Editor's note: Colson's surgery was successful, and he has had no recurrence of cancer.

Chapter Thirty-six

Playing It Safe Is Just Playing

The letters I receive from readers range from encouraging to scathing. They are . . . well . . . invigorating. At times, I confess, I have wondered why I don't stay on safe ground, writing about devotional topics rather than controversial issues like terrorism and the Supreme Court.

But that's just the point. If Christianity is true, then it bears on every aspect of life—and we must seek to examine all things temporal in light of the eternal. If we confine our faith to just "spiritual" topics, we begin to think inwardly, talk only to ourselves, and make little impact on our world.

I think there is a tendency to do just that. Several years ago a Christian friend, the editor of a major U.S. newspaper, told me he had added several religion writers to his staff. "Look at the religion page," he enthused. "We're doubling the coverage!" He apparently believed that meant he was doubling his witness for Christ.

But just writing *about* religion is not the same as making a Christian impact on our culture. Pollsters tells us that fifty million Americans say they are born again. Evangelicals have come out of the closet in recent years, accompanied by a surge of Christian books, records, celebrities, and candidates.

No doubt about it, religion is up. But so are values unremittingly opposed to the truth of Christianity: One out of every two marriages shatters in divorce. One out of three pregnancies terminates in abortion. Homosexuality is no longer considered depravity, but an "alternative lifestyle." Crime continues to soar—in "Christian" America there are 100 times more burglaries than in "pagan" Japan.

That is the great paradox today: Sin abounds in the midst of unprecedented religiosity. If there are so many of us, why are we not affecting our world?

I believe it is because many Christians fall into the same trap my editor friend did. We compartmentalize our faith, treating it like a section of the newspaper. It is sandwiched in our schedules between relatives and running, one of many activities competing for our attention.

Not that we aren't serious about it. We spend time in prayer, worship, and weekly Bible studies. But, of course, we are serious about our jobs, fitness, and families as well.

British writer Harry Blamires addresses this dilemma in *The Christian Mind*. The typical believer, he says, works side by side with a secularist, prays sincerely about his work, but never talks candidly with his colleagues about what motivates his plans and policies—because he is in a secular environment. When it comes to his spiritual life, he feels comfortable evaluating that in a Biblical context.

The result is an artificial dichotomy between the sacred and the secular. On the one hand are "Christian" topics like spiritual growth or discipleship; we think Christianly about such things. On the other hand is the world at large—which we evaluate in secular terms.

This spiritual schizophrenia results in believers bouncing back and forth between their secular and Christian mentalities as the conversation changes from the stock market to sanctification.

Such categorizing would be logical if Christianity were nothing more than a moral code or a set of profound teachings. It would then be just another of life's disciplines, something like yoga, Alcoholics Anonymous, or self-help courses.

But Christianity asserts itself as the central fact of human history: The God who created man invaded the world in the person of Jesus Christ, died, was resurrected, ascended, and lives today, sovereign over all.

If this claim is valid—if Christianity is historically true (and, of course, it is)—then it is not simply a file drawer in our crowded lives. It is the central truth from which all behavior, relationships, and philosophy must flow.

Blamires describes our predicament well: "As a thinking being, the modern Christian has succumbed to secularization. He accepts religion—its morality, its worship, its spiritual culture; but he rejects the religious view of life, the view which sets all earthly issues within the context of the eternal."

And as a result of our failure to apply Christian truth to all of life, the secular mind-set enjoys a virtually unchallenged monopoly in the forum of public debate.

In March 1986 the *Journal of the American Medical Association* published "On the Physical Death of Jesus Christ," an article describing the medical causes of Christ's death. Within days the magazine received an avalanche of angry letters attacking it for publishing religious material. One writer accused the journal of "disguising theological, we dare say, fundamentalist biases."

This seems a rather hysterical response to what few, Christian or pagan alike, would discount as historical fact. Whether He was the Son of God or not—the article did not assert Christ was resurrected—there was a historical figure named Jesus who was crucified. But the reaction illustrates how defensive secularists can become when their monopoly on the mainstream of cultural communications is challenged.

The problem is, we Christians allow this reaction to intimidate us. We withdraw from the fray, spending most of our time talking only to each other. We fail to bring the Christian mind to bear against the prevailing secular assumptions that define modern values.

But as Christian scholar and former president of the United Nations Charles Malik has said, "The problem is not only to win souls, but to save minds." We tend to venture out of our burrows only to conduct evangelistic outreaches; while we must preach the gospel, we must also seek to present a persuasive Christian view on the everyday issues of our culture.

This, then, is why I take pen in hand. If Christianity is true—as I fervently believe—then I must continue to explore the issues of the day, Bible in one hand and the morning's newspaper in the other.

Blamires sadly asserts, "There is no Christian mind." Nothing could more profoundly alter the character of our culture than for the millions who claim to be born again to prove him wrong.

October 1986

Chapter Thirty-seven

Friends of Religious Liberty: Why the Embarrassing Silence?

Jesus said that where one's treasure is, there will his heart be also. As I've studied two church-state cases recently, his words have come to mind. If we apply them to the way religious leaders reacted to these legal battles, we are left with some disturbing questions about the treasure—and heart—of the modern church.

The first case involved Sun Myung Moon, the famous founder of the heretical Unification Church. The U.S. government charged Moon with tax fraud in his failure to report interest on the nearly $2 million in his personal account, which he claimed he was merely holding for the church. Moon was also charged with obstructing justice by backdating documents and lying to the grand jury.

Representatives of several major denominations rallied to Moon's defense, testifying that it is common practice for pastors to hold funds on behalf of their churches. But the jury held that Moon used the funds for personal benefit, and found him guilty.

Church leaders expressed outrage, assailing the Internal Revenue Service for interfering with the free exercise clause of the Constitution. Respected evangelical groups such as the National Association of Evangelicals and the Christian Legal Society filed supporting briefs, as did many mainline churches and the Mormons. New Right groups with whom Moon has long been allied plunged in; so did the American Civil Liberties Union after Moon hired one of its favorite lawyers. The cause of religious liberty makes strange bedfellows these days.

But Moon lost his appeals. The self-proclaimed messiah was unceremoniously deposited in the federal prison in Danbury, Connecticut.

After his release he arrived in Washington to a hero's welcome. Full-page newspaper ads signed by many religious groups charged that Moon was persecuted for his faith. To this day Moon, and many religious groups, insist on his innocence.

I surely agree that the church should rise to the defense of anyone whose religious liberty is threatened. But I also find it ironic that Christian leaders fell all over themselves to ally with Moon, a blasphemous heretic who claims Christ's earthly ministry was aborted by the crucifixion, so he has now returned in the person of one Sun Myung Moon.

The other case was less celebrated. It involved a young woman named Marian Guinn, a divorced mother of four who moved to Collinsville, Oklahoma, in 1978 to live with her sister. She was soon introduced to the local Church of Christ, was baptized, and became a member.

Church members warmly received Guinn, testifying for her at custody hearings, driving her children to doctor's appointments, and eventually even giving her a car.

But then Guinn began living with the former mayor of Collinsville. She stopped attending church.

The elders begged her to end the illicit relationship and return to church. During their third meeting they warned that if she did not repent, an announcement would have to be made to the congregation, and fellowship withdrawn from her.

Guinn angrily tried to withdraw, but Church of Christ rules do not permit it. The elders removed her from membership and read a statement urging church members to pray for Guinn and to try to persuade her to repent and return.

Marian Guinn immediately filed suit for $1.3 million, alleging the church's actions invaded her privacy and produced emotional distress. (Should not the conviction of sin produce emotional distress?) Her attorney informed *Newsweek*, "I don't care if she fornicates up one side of the street and down the other, it's none of the church's business."

Incredibly, after a four-day trial the jury awarded Guinn $390,000; appeal is now pending. But no denomination has filed a supporting brief; no Christian groups have risen up in defense of religious liberty.

Perhaps what is not a priority for church bureaucrats is very important to ordinary church folk, however. Donations have come to Collinsville from lay people across the country—$900,000 in small checks and crumpled bills. That's enough, the church elders say, to pay costs if their appeal is lost, so they have started to return additional contributions. (That is newsworthy by itself.)

Let's look at the issues in these two cases. According to Moon and his supporters, at stake was a church or pastor's right to control church money, free from government intrusion. (It should be noted, however, that the evidence was convincing that Moon kept control for his personal benefit.)

One of the jurors in the Guinn case summed up its central issue when he said indignantly, "I don't see that it's the church's business to tell people how to live." In other words, can a church insist that its members live by Biblical standards of righteousness?

Does the greater threat to religious freedom in this country involve how we handle Mammon or how we respect Biblical commandments of holiness? Jesus very clearly condemned obsession with money, but he devoted much of his teaching to the pursuit of righteousness.

Admittedly, the elders of the Collinsville Church of Christ are not as glamorous, rich, or politically well connected as the Reverend Moon. If they erred, perhaps it was on the side of too rigidly enforcing the Bible—but I have trouble faulting that. In any event, unlike the Moon case, there were no full-page ads in newspapers, no briefs filed, no national organizations formed to warn of threats to religious liberty.

Even if there is an issue of religious liberty in the Moon case, the threat in the Guinn case is demonstrably greater. If the U.S. government seized all of our bank accounts, it could not destroy the church; but if it successfully prevented the church from requiring that its members obey Biblical standards, we might as well close our doors.

So why the passionate defense of Moon and the embarrassed silence toward the Collinsville elders? One would hate to think that money, advertising, and powerful political connections are more important to church leaders than holiness.

April 1986

Chapter Thirty-eight

The Right to Lie

This month [November 1985] the Supreme Court hears unusual oral arguments in the case of convicted murderer Emmanuel Charles Whiteside, who contends his lawyer should have allowed him to lie in court.

Though the issues the case raises are complex, the facts are not: In February 1977 Whiteside fatally stabbed one Calvin Love. He told his attorney, Gary Robinson, that he did not see a weapon but "believed" Love had one.

Then just before his trial, Whiteside informed Robinson that he would testify he had seen something "metallic." "If I don't say I saw a gun, I'm dead," he explained. Robinson warned him that false testimony would be perjury, and if Whiteside gave it, Robinson would be forced to withdraw from the case and possibly testify against him.

As Whiteside now argues, he had no choice: He testified truthfully and was convicted.

Iowa courts threw out Whiteside's appeal that Robinson had denied him "effective representation." But a federal court found that attorney Robinson "impermissibly compromised" Whiteside's constitutional rights by "restricting" his testimony.

So Whiteside's *right*—in this case, to lie—was upheld over this lawyer's legal and moral *responsibility* to the judicial system. It is this conflict which the Supreme Court must now resolve—and in the process, perhaps, establish a constitutional "right" to lie.

The protection of individual rights—called "inalienable" in the Declaration of Independence—is a cherished tradition of American democracy and its chief bulwark against tyranny.

Rights do not exist in a vacuum, however; they beget corresponding responsibilities. The right of citizenship, for example, creates such responsibilities as taxes, jury duty, and service in the common defense. Democracy demands that this crucial balance be maintained.

But in America today the scales are tipping. We have come to regard the benefits of freedom as rights which are unencumbered by responsibility. And in our permissive society, just about anything anybody wants to do can be justified by calling it a right.

This obsession with rights has affected every area of life. Consider some recent examples:

On "Good Morning America" recently, Susan Baker, cofounder of a campaign to put warning labels on offensive rock music, cited records extolling everything from incest to satanic worship. A music critic glibly dismissed her concerns, shrugging, "You can't repeal the culture." The lead singer of a popular rock group added, "It's really an issue of rights. As a songwriter, I have a right to express myself."

It may not be fashionable to say this nowadays, but the First Amendment is not a blank check. As Oliver Wendell Holmes wrote, the right of free speech does not extend to shouting "Fire!" in a crowded theater. Nor does it include polluting the minds of a generation of young Americans.

In the recent drug cases involving professional athletes, many columnists have defended the offenders on grounds that what they snort or smoke in private is their personal right. What about their responsibility to millions of young people for whom they are heroes and role models?

A few years ago government assistance programs were called "grants" or "aid"—that is, benefits the government chose to incur. Today, however, they are "entitlements," which Webster defines as a "right to demand or expect." And a budget full of demanded rights cannot be cut—thus we are facing a $200 billion federal budget deficit.

A variety of special interest groups disguise their goals as rights. Thus, homosexuals contend not only for tolerance but for "gay rights." While it is wrong to discriminate, it would also be wrong to confer special civil rights for those engaging in immoral behavior.

If there is one inalienable right, it is the right to life; but note how cleverly pro-abortion forces have stolen the terminology with their claim of a woman's right to control her own body!

The lie is everywhere. It is as if by simply labeling something as a right, one is relieved of the moral consequences of one's actions.

The rebuttal, of course, should come from the church. The balance of rights with responsibilities is firmly rooted in Scripture. In ancient Israel, the right to harvest private crops carried with it a responsibility to leave gleanings for the poor. God's blessings were always coupled with commandments to care for others less fortunate. Jesus affirmed that to whom much is given, much is required.

But can we Christians expose this lie, or are we riddled with it ourselves? Much of our TV preaching and literature proclaims only the rights of being God's children: health, happiness, success, prosperity. The focus is on blessings rather than sacrifice, the rights of the Kingdom without reference to our responsibilities to the King.

As Christians enjoying freedoms known few other places in the world, we have a special call to speak a sobering word: Rights divorced from responsibilities are the seeds of destruction. Maybe the Iowa "right to lie" case, preposterous though it seems, will serve a worthy purpose if it jars us awake.

Edmund Burke, the eighteenth-century statesman, summed it up well: "Liberty without wisdom or responsibility . . . [is] . . . the greatest of all possible evils."

November 1985

Chapter Thirty-nine

On Waving Flags and Washing Feet

Shortly after I became a Christian, I experienced something of an identity crisis. Here I was—born again, a citizen of God's holy nation, yet still a citizen of the United States, a taxpayer, subject to the laws of the land. Was there a conflict?

One of the first books I read chronicled the Christian heritage of America. Tremendous. I had been a flag-waver all my life; nothing stirred my soul like "The Marine Hymn." What a wonderful discovery that God had been on my side all along.

But then I began to study Scripture and was unsettled to discover that we "worship another King" and are but "sojourners in this land." I read elsewhere how Hitler claimed his was the "chosen" race, invoking God to justify unspeakable horrors. God and country, I realized, could become an unholy alliance. I was torn.

At the same time, the old standard of "my country, right or wrong," had become, in Vietnam's wake, "my country, always wrong." For many, *patriotism* became a dirty word.

Happily, in recent years we seem to be recovering a sense of national purpose; but through the time of upheaval I suspect many

Christians questioned, as I did, whether one could be a patriot of the nation-state as well as a citizen of the Kingdom of God.

So [1986] as we prepare to celebrate the 210th birthday of our nation, perhaps it's time to consider anew whether there is such a thing as Christian patriotism.

Some make the mistake I did early in my Christian experience, believing there are only two options: marrying the flag and the cross, or completely separating the two.

But they can be neither married nor divorced. This is the distinct tension built into Christian citizenship. We cannot withdraw from the world and pretend we are somehow dwelling in Heaven now; nor can we embrace the world and assume earthly governments can be claimed for Christ. Both extremes are un-Biblical. We live, as Augustine put it, in two cities.

Augustine, however, reconciled this dual citizenship. One cannot love the whole world, practically speaking. But since God has placed us in a particular nation or circumstance, we can demonstrate our love for the world by paying "special regard" to those around us, being godly citizens of whatever kingdom we are in. If children, parents, kings, judges, taxpayers, and tax-collectors were all "that Christian religion has taught men should be," the result, Augustine argued, would be "the salvation of the commonwealth."

This, I believe, beautifully captures the essence of Christian responsibility within the state. We should be the most responsible citizens because we understand government is God's ordained structure to impose order and restrain sin in a fallen world. Within this structure, we are to love our neighbors, be light and leaven, pray for those in authority and obey them—up to the point that the government demands an allegiance higher than God, or commands practices contrary to His Word.

This responsibility of Christian citizenship was well expressed by a Nepali pastor imprisoned for preaching the gospel, which is against the law in his Hindu nation. "Of course I must obey my Lord and spread His Word," he said during a recent visit to the U.S.

"But even though we are persecuted, we who are Christians in Nepal pride ourselves on being the best citizens our king has. We try to be faithful to the fullest extent we can. We love our country—but we love our God more."

C. S. Lewis offers the analogy of the family to illustrate how the Christian loves his country. One doesn't love family members only when they are good; rather, we seek lovingly to correct their faults. So, too, the Christian can remain faithful to country while weeping over and seeking to correct its faults.

The latter is the key point. Because he knows his ultimate accountability is to God, the Christian remains faithful to country, but without suspending his moral judgment. Indeed, it is the addition of moral judgment to political allegiance that makes patriotism responsible. Lutheran pastor Richard Neuhaus sums it up well: "Loyalty to the *civitas* can safely be nurtured only if the *civitas* is not the object of highest loyalty."

The Christian patriot recognizes that the phrase "one nation under God" is not a license for blind, arrogant nationalism, but rather a humbling acknowledgment that a people live under the judgment of God.

This perhaps explains why John Adams wrote that a patriot must be a "religious man." The Christian's faith calls him to civic duty—knowing the needs of neighbors and meeting them, demonstrating faith with works of charity. The Christian patriot, after all, spends more time washing feet than waving flags. And in flags he sees symbols, not of military or economic might, but of the common good of the specific people a sovereign God has given him to serve.

That's patriotism in its place, a patriotism worth singing about—and even dying for.

June 1986

PART IV

Prisons and Criminal Justice

Chapter Forty

You Can't Cure the Wilding Sickness

These are violent days in America, and wherever I go I'm asked about it. Why is the crime rate out of control? Why is common decency so uncommon? When mayhem becomes mundane in a so-called civilized land, what can stem the tide?

The questions intensified after the now infamous "wilding"—the senseless crime in New York's Central Park that left us all shocked and outraged.

Few people are unfamiliar with the facts of the case. The young investment banker had been warned about jogging by herself at night; but, as a friend remembered, "She was the kind who said, 'Why would anybody want to hurt me?'"

But a group of boys between the ages of fourteen and seventeen did want to hurt her. There was no special reason. She was raped, stabbed, beaten, and left for dead. Somehow she survived.

New York police are familiar with gangs, drugs, neglect, abuse, and how young people from such backgrounds can turn on others. But these kids were a bit different. They lived on the edge of Harlem, to be sure. But four of the youths lived in a building that had a doorman. One was enrolled in parochial school. Another had just received an *A* on a book report. Another played the tuba in his school band. These kids were frighteningly normal.

They were normal—except that none voiced any remorse about the crime. In jail the boys joked about the attack as if they were boasting of video-game victories.

Every commentary on this horrific case asks the same question I'm so often asked: *Why?*

Some answers are as outrageous as the crime itself. Forensic psychologist Shawn Johnston explained that the boys are "damaged . . . in pain inside . . . acting out their pain on innocent victims." As Harvard educator Alvin Poussaint put it, "They're letting out anger. There's a lot of free-floating anger and rage among a lot of our youth." And psychologist Richard Majors summed up, "We have to be honest. Society has not been nice to these kids."

So these boys are only victims of our not-so-nice society—not depraved, just deprived?

Well, the usual psycho-socio babble doesn't work here. Bad influences may well be at work in these youths' lives, but as *Washington Post* columnist Haynes Johnson observed, those allegedly involved "did not come from the classic 'pathology of poverty' background that is supposed to be a sociological breeding ground for violence and criminality."

But why would "good" kids do such a terrible thing?

I think I know.

During a recent trip to Europe, I met with a psychiatrist in a model correctional institution. She explained how 71 percent of the inmates there had been classified as mentally abnormal, or psychiatric cases, since they had committed particularly heinous crimes. Since people are inherently good, the doctor inferred, anyone who does evil must be mentally ill. So inmates with this "illness" were sent to her institution to be "cured."

While mental illnesses can generate horrible crimes, we cannot label all violent acts as manifestations of madness. Thus I was skeptical of the psychiatrist's claims. And just a few days after my visit, my skepticism was horribly borne out.

Part of the "cure" for one inmate, a convicted rapist, was a short furlough under the escort of a twenty-six-year-old female guard. Prison officials evidently considered it therapeutic for him to attend a movie with a woman, a step on his road to "normalcy." He didn't get very far down that road. Instead, not far from the prison gates, the inmate battered and murdered the young woman.

Violent tendencies are not an illness. Criminal behaviors are not symptoms of a disease. We cannot explain away awful acts through sociological factors or odd chromosomes or poverty or germs or drugs. While these can surely be factors in criminal behavior, the root cause of crime has not changed since Cain.

It is sin.

The Bible teaches that men and women's natures are inherently depraved. Without restraints, sin will emerge and wreak its havoc on whatever crosses its path. And we surely live in an age in which traditional restraints have crumbled.

Reports on the Central Park case have cited the "randomness" of the gang's attacks. Before the group accosted the lone woman jogger, they had already assaulted at least six other people and thrown rocks at cars and bicyclists. As one reporter put it, they attacked "anything that moved."

Random violence, devoid of motive or meaning, is supremely chilling. It is also supremely logical. If man is not created by God in God's image, if human beings and their environment are simply the result of random collisions of atoms, there is no intrinsic distinction between "good" and "evil" human behaviors, and people have no innate value. ("She was nothing," said one of the alleged rapists about his victim.) So perhaps these boys are actually existential purists bent on living out the consequences of their belief system.

This means that for the rest of us, braving Central Park is a game of chance. You can jog along on East Drive, take a left at 102nd Street, and if the park animals get you, that's the roll of the dice. A young New York girl described the jogger's losing spin on the roulette wheel this way: "It is like she committed suicide."

One cannot listen to the evening news in America today

without being assured daily of the existence of evil. Sometimes, as in the Central Park attack, its perpetrators are frighteningly normal. They're kids who write book reports and smile at the doorman and play the tuba.

But even as the dichotomy between their normality and their evil terrifies us, we should not be surprised. If there is no God and people are but randomly created beings, moral decisions are equally random.

As Dostoyevski wrote, if there is no God, then everything is lawful—and the highest law is the law of the self. As the Central Park case reminds us, that is the law of the jungle.

September 1989

Chapter Forty-one

God Speaking to the World from the Prisons

At a recent gathering, an elegantly dressed woman took my arm. Introducing herself as a member of a well-known suburban church, she said excitedly, "I've followed Prison Fellowship's ministry for years. I've been so inspired—in fact, I've started a small foundation working with inner-city churches. We're supplying food and clothing for people in need, helping young people find jobs. It's been so wonderful!"

She rushed away. I later learned that this woman, a person one might expect to be more comfortable conducting church teas, was leading a major campaign bringing suburban church resources to work in ghetto areas.

Later her words echoed in my mind. I thought of countless similar encounters during Prison Fellowship's history. Often God has used this ministry as a catalyst for motivating His people.

Political leaders have become concerned about prisoners. Hundreds of churches have opened their doors to the needy; thousands of volunteers have opened their homes to inmates and their families. One couple wrote me recently that they had been "nominal" Christians, but after participating in two in-prison seminars, they had discovered Christ and were "on fire for the Lord."

God has undeniably used Prison Fellowship. But why? Why would He use prisons, places of utter powerlessness, to powerfully impact society?

While reflecting on these questions, I happened to be reading the celebrated memoirs of the Cuban poet Armando Valladares. His book turned out to be one of the most powerful I've read. In its riveting pages, I found answers to my questions.

Valladares was twenty-three when he was arrested in 1960 for opposing Castro. He spent twenty-two years in prison; his book, *Against All Hope*, exposes the unspeakable brutality he and his fellow prisoners endured.

During one three-month period, they were given showers of human urine and excrement by sadistic guards. Each night Valladares would hear condemned men marched outside. Then he would hear shouts of "*Viva Cristo Rey!*—Long live Christ the King!"—just before exploding rifle fire shattered their defiant cries.

Valladares had come to prison a nominal believer, but with all else stripped away, he discovered the living Christ. He wrote, "His presence made my faith an indestructible shield."

But Valladares's testimony reveals more than the indestructibility of faith. Just as Solzhenitsyn's *Gulag Archipelago* exposed the horrors of Soviet oppression, so this book from a Cuban prison exposed Castro's ruthless regime to the world.

Castro had been able to take over the press, win the allegiance of the masses, control the bureaucracy, and even co-opt the church. His totalitarian regime successfully subdued every institution of Cuban culture except one—the prisons.

A *Washington Post* critic wrote: "Valladares's report from a revolution's heart of darkness . . . brought the West's consciousness to a new place. The price paid by Cuba's legions of political prisoners, who have made Castro the leading jailer in the world, is finally becoming clear. The person most responsible for this change is Armando Valladares. . . ."

Thus it is through the voices of Christian prisoners honoring Christ as King that God speaks to the world. It is a pattern one discovers throughout history.

Joseph was lifted out of prison to become prime minister of Egypt. Jeremiah was imprisoned for his preaching—but he kept on prophetically challenging God's people. Virtually every one of the disciples spent time in prison; many of the Apostle Paul's most stirring words were written from a Roman cell.

John Bunyan wrote the great classic *Pilgrim's Progress* from jail. Dostoyevsky's prison experience led to the powerful Christian message in his writings. German martyr Dietrich Bonhoeffer wrote from a Nazi prison; similarly, from Corrie ten Boom's concentration-camp sufferings came rich wisdom. And the monumental work of Alexander Solzhenitsyn emerged from years in the Soviet gulag.

Why does God use prisons in such a way?

Perhaps because His heart is drawn inexorably to the suffering and oppressed. In Scripture Christ enjoins His church to care for the hungry, the sick, the naked, the imprisoned. As Cardinal Sin reminded our Prison Fellowship International leaders at the Nairobi Convocation in 1986, we draw power as a ministry not because of who we are, but because of the people to whom we minister—the suffering for whom our God has a special compassion.

In addition, prison forces total dependence on God. Valladares wrote that when all hope was gone, he thrust himself into the waiting arms of Christ. Solzhenitsyn wrote that only when he surrendered all power in prison did he discover real freedom.

And for those of us imprisoned in less hostile regimes, prison is the place where all else—pleasures, possessions, distractions—is stripped away. Prison magnifies God's still, small voice; in human weakness, His strength is revealed.

Prison Fellowship's decade of ministry certainly follows this pattern. This ministry was born and raised in prison. Its initial vision came when I saw God's power so clearly in the Christian inmates around me. The vision became a reality when Federal

Prison Director Norman Carlson suddenly allowed us to furlough inmates from prison for discipleship seminars.

What caused Carlson to take such an unprecedented risk? Not political influence or my persuasive powers, but the impact of an unknown inmate's prayer for him a few weeks earlier in a prison chapel.

Our in-prison seminars began in a similar way. In 1977, when we wanted to furlough a Christian inmate from prison to attend a Washington seminar, Warden George Ralston flatly refused. "If you guys are so good," he challenged, "why don't you bring your teaching team into our prison?"

So we did. Not in triumphal strength, but with our knees knocking—and God used that first attempt to launch a program that after ten years of ministry [1987] has reached 91,000 inmates with the gospel.

Internationally, the pattern has been the same. Appianda Arthur, deputy minister of justice in Ghana, was jailed when his government was toppled by a Marxist coup. In prison he read *Born Again*, and the Holy Spirit began to work on his heart. Today he is free, a fervent Christian, and regional director of Prison Fellowship in Africa.

John Lee was a successful Singaporean attorney when he was assigned by the court to defend a death-row prisoner. The prisoner was known as the meanest man in the prison—but when John met him, he had been utterly transformed by Christ. The encounter soon turned John's life upside-down: He closed his law practice and is today our Southeast Asia director.

God clearly has a special use for the prisons, both in our ministry and beyond. He confounds man's wisdom: on the one hand challenging Castro's tyranny from the writings of a half-dead prisoner; on the other, challenging comfortable Christians in affluent churches to new heights of faith—from this ministry among forgotten prisoners.

The power of this movement is that it has grown not from the top down, but from the bottom up. Its remarkable impact has come not from Chuck Colson, not from a fine organizational structure, money, or the backing of evangelical and political leaders. Rather, it has come from God speaking to His world today. And He speaks, as He has through the centuries, from the most unlikely place—the prisons.

February 1987

Chapter Forty-two

The Day I Was Taken Back to Prison

Often God gets our attention when we least expect it.

It happened to me recently. I was at a luncheon for about twenty-five Prison Fellowship supporters. One of our instructors, Larry Yarrington, was to speak. I had met Larry just once, but I knew from reports that inmates by the dozens came to know Christ in his In-Prison Seminars.

Larry is tall, dark-haired; with a strong jaw, he is the picture of confidence. A Ph.D. and business executive, he seemed perfect to address this group. I settled back, ready for him to dazzle us with stories of dramatic conversions.

But as Larry began, I started to feel uneasy. He didn't talk about the glories of our seminars. Instead, he spoke slowly and deliberately: "I'd like to share from the heart today. I'd like to share what goes on inside of a prisoner. I'd like to give you a sense of that—because I was once a prisoner."

I hadn't known Larry had served time. He went on to talk about his feelings of rejection, rooted in childhood by a demanding and domineering father. He had compensated by excelling in school, in business, in whatever he took on. But it never had been enough.

Then he had ended up going to prison—where his sense of worthlessness was reinforced.

He described his recurring feelings of inadequacy: "It's as if I'm
a stranger at a party, dressed in shabby clothes," he said.
"Meanwhile all the other guests know one another and are all
dressed in tuxedos."

Wait a minute, I thought. Larry was not following the accepted
public relations script. *Tell us about the seminars*, I said under my
breath. *Our supporters don't need to hear all this.*

My unease grew to near-panic as Larry explained that he still
felt a deep insecurity, even after his conversion; for whatever reason,
God had not seen fit to remove it. *What is he doing?* I muttered to
myself. *Christians are supposed to conquer their weaknesses—and
this man's a leader . . .*

Then came the unexpected. As Larry was explaining how he
felt like one of the inmates every time he taught a seminar, I suddenly forgot about the others in the room. Overwhelmed by long-
dormant memories, I was back in prison: Dormitory G at the
Maxwell Federal Prison in Montgomery, Alabama. I could smell it;
I felt the horrible loss of freedom and identity. I could look around
and see the men lying on their bunks, alone and helpless.

And I remembered the visiting days; I would stand on the
wrong side of the fence and watch visitors arrive. Other inmates'
attorneys would come in, immaculately dressed, leather briefcases
in hand. And I, former special counsel to the President of the United
States, now in my baggy brown dungarees and surplus prison shoes,
would stand aside to let them pass.

It was not only the irony of "how the mighty have fallen."
Trading freedom for prison had been a crushing exchange. And
because I had experienced it, I had *known* how my fellow inmates
felt—the deep sense of loneliness and worthlessness that incarcera-
tion breeds.

I also remembered that after my release, when I had returned
to speak in prisons across the U.S. and around the world, I had felt
that instant identification with the inmates. But subtly, as the years

had gone by, that sense of solidarity had begun to fade. And I hadn't even noticed. I still felt a passion for prisoners to come to Christ, a deep love and urgency to help them—but I had lost the vivid sense of being *one of them.* Larry Yarrington's words were reawakening it.

I tried to dry my eyes without anyone noticing. Then I glanced around the table only to find the others, including the chairman of one of America's largest corporations, doing the same thing. As Larry finished, they began to share their own hidden struggles. The luncheon became a remarkable time of deep sharing, prayer, and praise.

Why was Larry's story so powerful?

First, because of his refreshing honesty. So often we Christians are unwilling to admit any kind of weakness. It's as if we're afraid people won't believe we're spiritual enough, so we put on the mask of supersainthood. No worries, no warts, no weakness. Yet when we honestly acknowledge our shortcomings, as Larry showed us, our transparency breaks down barriers and draws us to one another.

Second, Larry's talk was a poignant lesson in the most profound Biblical paradox: It is in our weakness that God's strength is perfected. What made Larry such an outstanding seminar leader was precisely his sense of inadequacy. Just as God had not removed Paul's "thorn in the flesh," so too He had chosen not to remove Larry's insecurity. But that weakness turned out to be the very key to his ability to relate to inmates.

But there was a third reason—for me, at least—that Larry's talk was so powerful. Though I had vowed I would never forget how it felt to be an inmate, I had. Caught up in speaking, writing, and leadership responsibilities to the Christian world, I had lost a sense of real identification with the powerless. But that day at lunch Larry Yarrington brought me back to prison. And that's where I belong.

December 1988

Chapter Forty-three

A Way of Escape at San Quentin

I relearned a few lessons recently [1989] at a tough, old prison called San Quentin.

We had been planning my visit there for months. Out of the prison's 2,200 inmates, more than 300 had signed up for our Prison Fellowship chapel service, and I was excited about the grand opportunity to preach the gospel in this rough place.

Just days before our visit, however, officials uncovered a hidden cache of weapons and a potentially violent plot. The prison was immediately locked down, with inmates confined to their cells twenty-four hours a day.

When we arrived, the lockdown was still in effect. I asked if I could at least walk the blocks: five tiers of small, thick-barred cells with narrow catwalks along the outer walls. Guards in towers along the perimeter could keep their rifles trained on every cell.

Usually prisons are raucous with the sounds of television, shouting, scuffling feet, clanging steel doors. On this day there was silence.

We went on to the chapel, where a group of PF volunteers and honor-camp inmates were waiting. They were mostly Christians.

I was glad to see them, of course, but I was also disheartened. This had been my opportunity to preach the gospel to hardened offenders. Now I felt I was preaching to the choir.

I struggled with my lack of enthusiasm. *Maybe I'll just give a short devotional, ten minutes or so*, I thought. *I can't really preach my heart out to this crowd.*

But then I noticed a video camera in the far end of the room. *Perhaps this is being recorded for the chapel library. Maybe I'd better give it my all.*

And as I started to speak, spurred on by the eye of the camera, I suddenly felt the Holy Spirit's conviction. I remembered I was called by God to preach His Word, no matter if one inmate or a thousand were listening.

I preached with more and more fervor, telling the inmates about the Christ who loved them even in that stronghold of violence and despair.

Afterwards I mentioned to the chaplain how disappointed I was that I wasn't able to give my message to the men on lockdown. He looked surprised. "Didn't you know?" he said. "Because of the lockdown, the administration agreed to videotape your sermon. They'll be showing it to all the inmates tomorrow on closed-circuit TV in the morning and again in the afternoon."

I was overwhelmed. Because of the lockdown, 2,200 prisoners would hear the gospel. God had arranged a far more effective way for far more inmates to hear His Word. Yet, if I had not been faithful to preach it, the opportunity would have been missed. (And, I found out later, the prison administration aired the sermon not just twice, but nearly a dozen times over the following weeks!)

To me, the lessons were threefold.

The first is Mother Teresa's simple truth: *God calls us to faithfulness, not success.* We are motivated not by flattering statistics or amazing testimonies—though we strive for good stewardship and are thrilled when inmates come to know Christ and we can tell their stories to His glory.

No, our goal is simply obedience. God has called me and an

army of Christian volunteers to bring His light to places of darkness like San Quentin, His love to places of need like the homes of inmates' families. We are to do it no matter what happens—or doesn't happen—around us.

The second lesson is a paradox: When we set the full-scale changing of a prison, or of society itself, as our goal, we most often fail. But when we set obedience to God as our goal, He blesses those efforts in ways we could never envision.

As it turns out, Prison Fellowship's area director in San Francisco tells me my visit opened the door for our ministry to begin a variety of new Christian programs in that prison. My one-time visit, in which nothing went as *I* had planned, was used by God for *His* plan to open up a new, regular, sustained ministry at San Quentin.

A third lesson extends to our mission as Christians to our society at large.

As I write this, many are feeling a sense of weariness and frustration. We throw ourselves into whatever ministry God has called us to—and yet the needs facing us are intractable. The forces of secularism, moral decay, poverty, homelessness, hunger, crime, and injustice sometimes seem overwhelming.

The temptation is to give up, to retreat to the safer ground of church suppers and choir practice. The problems seem so dismaying; our small efforts feel so draining. At San Quentin I was weary in well-doing—not because of a lack of conviction, but because sustained energy over the long haul can take a toll.

This is why we must bear one another's burdens, why we must help one another when we faint. And we know that the One on whom we wait will not allow us to stumble, but will renew our strength.

And this is why we must each do our part. My part that day at San Quentin was to preach. As he carries the baton forward, our San Francisco area director will work hard to instill PF programs. The volunteers who follow will bring their love to inmates and their families, who will in turn touch others. God will work His will through those efforts.

So we must not waver. What our nation needs most right now is a movement of people motivated not by short-term success, but by obedience, demonstrating a holy perseverance that only God Himself can give.

These are simple lessons, after all. But oddly enough, without the eye of a television camera on that locked-down day in San Quentin, I might not have remembered them. It is evidence yet again that in the face of temptation God always provides "a way of escape."

March 1989

Chapter Forty-four

The Celebrity Illusion

"What can I do about it? I'm just an ordinary person."
That is the despairing refrain I often hear in response to problems ranging from world hunger to crime. Most people simply feel impotent when it comes to big issues.

Considering what we hear from politicians and the media, this widespread attitude is not surprising. We have been conditioned to believe that all problems must have a government solution—or that one must be famous before one can make any significant impact on society.

This political/celebrity illusion has become the dominant myth of our times. And few have embraced it with more enthusiasm than the Christian community. We seem to think we need a big parachurch organization or a well-known celebrity in order to accomplish anything for the Kingdom of God. As a result, the church has elevated popular pastors, ministry leaders, and televangelists to the dubious pedestal of fame—only to watch many topple in the winds of power, influence, and adulation. All the while, "ordinary" Christians feel more and more frustrated.

One reason I enjoy going to the Third World regularly is that this paralyzing myth does not hold sway there. In the face of human needs and social problems, Christians cannot count on government, since it is far more likely to persecute than listen to the church; there are few parachurch organizations at work; and there are no Christian celebrities. So these "poor, deprived" Christians have no alternative but to go ahead and do what needs doing. And that turns out to be just what the Bible commands.

A friend of mine from Madagascar provides an example. Pascal, a university professor, was thrown into prison after a Marxist coup. There he became a Christian.

After his release he started a small import/export company. But he was drawn back to his prison to preach the gospel. During one such visit in early 1986, he stopped in shock as he passed the infirmary: there were more than fifty corpses piled on the veranda, naked except for ID tags between their toes.

Pascal went to the nurse, asking if there had been an epidemic. Of sorts, he was told. Prisoners were dying by the dozens—of malnutrition.

Pascal left the prison in tears. His church was too poor to help feed the starving inmates, and there were no big relief agencies around. So he began to do what he could, cooking meals in his own small kitchen. Today Pascal and his wife continue to cook—and without the benefit of a government agency or Christian organization they are making the difference between life and death for 700 prisoners.

Of all people, Christians should know better than to buy into the illusion that change comes only through Congress or celebrity campaigns. God has always used the humble both to confound the wisdom of this world and to accomplish His purposes. Much of the Bible was, after all, written by the powerless—prisoners, exiles, and part-time shepherds who were prophets.

God continues today to turn the world's expectations upside-down, using ordinary Christians to make the difference. One experience in particular brought that point home to me.

Following the National Prayer Breakfast [1987], I took a

group of supporters to Maryland's Jessup institution where a Prison Fellowship in-prison seminar was in progress. We were welcomed by the bright lights of TV cameras. Reporters scribbled notes while officials greeted us warmly; the governor had even issued a proclamation for the occasion.

By the time we got to the prison chapel, it was on the verge of exploding with the excitement of more than 125 inmates and dozens of PF volunteers. Wintley Phipps, a well-known gospel singer who had sung only the day before for President Reagan, was with us. When Wintley let loose in that cinder-block chapel, the walls shook.

Then my colleague Herman Heade, who was converted in a solitary-confinement cell during a seven-year prison term, gave his testimony. He was dramatic and convicting.

The excitement continued as I then challenged the men to accept Christ. When the time came to leave, we could barely make our way through the crowd. Inmates pressed around, hugging us and weeping. It would be hard to find a more powerful church service anywhere.

The next day our seminar instructor was relieved to find all the inmates had returned for the seminar's final session. He had thought the last day might be anticlimactic.

At the closing meeting, a tall inmate stood to speak. "I really appreciated Chuck Colson's message," he told the group, "and Wintley Phipps's singing stirred me beyond words. Herman's testimony reached me right where I was at.

"Frankly, though, those things really didn't impress me so much as what happened after all the celebrities and TV cameras left: the ladies among the volunteers went into the dining hall, with all the noise and confusion, and sat at the table to have a meal with us. That's what really got to me," he concluded, his voice choked.

What was the witness of Christ at the Maryland prison? Certainly Wintley's singing and Herman's testimony and my sermon were appreciated. But the most powerful message came from the volunteers—ordinary people whose names never appear in the headlines—who went into the dingy dining hall to share a prison meal with the inmates.

In spite of the myth of our times, it does not take celebrities or institutions to make a difference. The improbable way God builds His Kingdom is through those who follow His example of sacrifice—as Pascal and those unknown volunteers at Jessup prison prove so beautifully.

This is an appropriate time of year [Christmas] to be thinking about these things, for they explain a great deal about Christ's life and ministry. After all, His royal birth was marked not by pomp and power, but by the wonder of peasants who glimpsed His hidden glory. He came to serve, not to be served, to reach out to the lowly, the suffering, the weak, and the oppressed. He surrounded Himself with ordinary people whose lives He utterly transformed. And in turn the world has been changed by their witness of His power.

December 1987

Chapter Forty-five

Victims and Victimizers

Several months ago [1989] *The Washington Post* published a story that shocked the capital city. A woman named Pamela Small recounted her experience as a crime victim. One day in 1973 while Small was shopping at an import store, the manager turned on her, smashed her skull with a hammer, and slit her throat. She somehow survived.

Her attacker, nineteen-year-old John Mack, was convicted and sentenced to fifteen years in prison. He served about two years in a county jail, then was paroled—partially because he had a job awaiting him with a Texas congressman.

Over the years Mack's boss rose in seniority. So did Mack. Congressman Jim Wright eventually became Speaker of the House, and John Mack his top aide. And soon after Pamela Small's public reflections on her personal ordeal, both toppled.

Most observers have focused on whether or not Mack served a sufficient sentence.

But I believe all the bile directed at John Mack is misplaced. Though Mack undoubtedly should have repented and asked Pamela Small's forgiveness—which Small said would have helped her deal with the crime—he did serve time and rebuild his life. And I, for one, would be loathe to discourage the restoration of an ex-offender.

No, our outrage should instead be directed at our criminal justice system—a system indicted by the attitude of former Representative Tony Coelho: "Under our system of law John Mack owed his debt to society, not to this young woman."

As a lawbreaker John Mack surely owed a debt to society. But to dispense real justice, our system must do more than punish the offender. It must seek to restore the victim. This used to be the case. Roman and early Anglo-Saxon law as well as Judeo-Christian codes held offenders responsible to repay their victims. The view that crime is primarily an offense against individuals became a well-established tradition in Western societies.

But in the Middle Ages, King Henry I issued laws that made himself the victim in criminal cases. Punishments were no longer viewed as ways of restoring victims but as means of redressing "injury" to the king.

Henry I is long gone, but his legacy is still with us. And stories like Pamela Small's remind us it is time for a change.

Change begins with remembering that crime not only breaks society's law, it injures individuals. A just, effective system will help restore victims, involving them in the criminal justice process while punishing criminals and maintaining order.

For some time now, Justice Fellowship has been advocating four principles to attain this goal.

First, victims should have the right to pursue civil damages as part of the criminal case. Financial reparation cannot begin to pay a crime's emotional toll. But monetary damages at least recognize a debt owed by the offender to the victim and require that it be paid.

Second, offenders who are not dangerous should be sentenced to restitution and community service-based punishments. Currently, to ease serious prison overcrowding, some violent offenders are released early to free cells for newcomers. Instead, nondangerous inmates—nearly half of the prison population—should be put to work in communities, paying their debt to society and making money to repay their victims.

Third, we must strengthen the many excellent victim assistance programs throughout the country. Churches need to help. The Good Samaritan parable is the story of a crime victim; today's church must be obedient to Christ's mandate to love victimized neighbors in the same way.

Fourth, we must expand victim-offender reconciliation programs, in which victims and offenders agree to meet face to face. For victims, these meetings are often a satisfying outlet for their anger, fear, and frustration; they realize that a person, not a monster, committed the offense. Offenders can realize the human impact of their crime, often asking for forgiveness. Both parties usually feel a sense of resolution and restoration, as excellent pilot programs such as South Carolina's VICTOR have demonstrated.

As Pamela Small's story reminds us, crime is not just an offense against "society," despite what Congressman Coelho says. It wounds real people, people who are too often ignored by our current system and by those who fail to differentiate between offenders and those they victimize. Consider Congressman Steny Hoyer's reaction after public outcry caused John Mack to resign: "There was a tragedy on both sides. Now that tragedy has been compounded."

As George Will wrote of this ridiculous observation, "The word 'tragedy' is just one of those puffy dumplings of words that tumble together in jumbles of blather when politicians . . . turn on their spigots of sententiousness. . . . Someone who speaks facilely of tragedy on all sides really sees it as none."

The ministry of Justice Fellowship is committed to the restoration of offenders, to introducing them to the forgiveness found in Jesus Christ and the new life He can bring. But our love for offenders does not cause us to blur the line between the offender and the one offended. To do so not only mocks justice itself, it further injures someone already bruised or broken by crime.

August 1989

Chapter Forty-six

Prisons and Punishment: I

After I addressed a state legislature, advocating alternatives to prison for nonviolent offenders, a bewildered representative accosted me: "As a fellow conservative, Mr. Colson, how can you be *against* punishment?"

It's a question I'm often asked—and a telling commentary on the practice of so many who consider prison and punishment synonymous. This serious confusion can undermine our most basic concepts of justice.

As a Christian, I most certainly believe in punishment. Biblical justice demands that individuals be held accountable. Throughout the history of ancient Israel, to break God's law was to invite swift, specific, and certain punishment. When a law was broken, the resulting imbalance could be righted only when the transgressor was punished and thus made to "pay" for his wrong.

Though modern sociologists take offense at this elemental concept of retribution, it is essential: If justice means getting one's due, then justice is denied when deserved punishment is not received. And ultimately this undermines one's role as a moral, responsible human being.

C. S. Lewis summed this up in his brilliant essay "The Humanitarian Theory of Punishment," which assails the view that lawbreakers should be "cured" or "treated" rather than punished. "To be punished, however severely, because we have deserved it, because we 'ought to have known better,' is to be treated as a human person made in God's image," says Lewis. In this Biblical sense, punishment is not only just, it is very often redemptive—to the offender, the victim, and society at large.

This is why the distinction between prison and punishment is so crucial. Prisons, though necessary to confine violent offenders, can hardly be considered redemptive.

And while punishment is clearly Biblical, American penal philosophy is not based on the Biblical principle of just deserts that Lewis cited; it is founded on a humanistic view that crime is an illness to be cured.

The pattern for American prisons was established two centuries ago when well-meaning Quakers converted Philadelphia's Walnut Street jail into a facility where offenders were confined in order to repent and be rehabilitated.

Though a number of those early "penitents" simply went mad, the idea caught on and flourished. Soothed by the comforting illusion that these miscreants were in reality being "treated," the public conscience could ignore the harsh conditions of their confinement. Thus such places came to be called not prisons, but *penitent*iaries, *reform*atories, and *correct*ional institutions.

This illusion was reinforced in the twentieth century when a school of liberal sociologists argued that crime was not the individual's fault, but society's. Societal failures like poverty, racism, and unemployment were to blame.

Former Attorney General Ramsey Clark summed up this fashionable view when he asserted unequivocally that poverty is "the cause of crime." President Carter echoed it when he blamed ghetto conditions for widespread looting during New York's 1977 power blackout.

If the criminal was but a victim of the system, prisons were therefore places for him or her to be vocationally trained, "socialized," and educated. Society, which had caused the disease of crime, would now cure it—and so ever-increasing thousands were packed into institutions as wards of the state.

Thus two centuries of the "humanitarian tradition" left America with more than one half million of its citizens incarcerated—the third largest per-capita prison population in the world—as well as the staggering recidivism statistics of the 1970s: 74 percent of ex-prisoners rearrested within four years of release. Prisons proved themselves not places of rehabilitation, but breeding grounds for further crime.

It's a travesty that in this so-called Christian nation we consistently ignore the most basic of Christ's teaching: sin comes from within the individual (Mark 7:20). It can't be foisted off on germs, genes, a bad neighborhood, or some impersonal entity called society.

Crime is the result of morally responsible people making wrong moral decisions, for which they must be held accountable. The just and necessary response to such behavior is redemptive punishment, which may include, as the Bible prescribes, restitution or community service, stiff fines, loss of rights, or in cases where the offender is dangerous, prison. But let's not kid ourselves any longer. Prison isn't to cure the individual. It's to lock him or her up.

President Reagan got to the heart of the issue in his 1981 speech to police chiefs of the nation:

> Controlling crime . . . is . . . ultimately a moral dilemma—one that calls for moral, or if you will, a spiritual solution. . . . The war on crime will be won only when our attitude of mind and a change of heart takes place in America, when certain truths take hold again and plant their roots deep in our national consciousness, truths like: right and wrong matters; individuals are responsible for their actions; retribution should be swift and sure for those who prey on the innocent.

But we continue building more prisons and filling them up. Why? Because public passions discern no difference between prisons and punishment. As long as that mind-set flourishes, the Biblical concept of justice cannot. And it will be society which will suffer the real punishment: $80,000 per cell for new prison construction, and spiraling crime and recidivism rates as well.

August 1985

Chapter Forty-seven

Prisons and Punishment: II

This has been a bad year [1985] for prison disturbances. Every month headlines report violence in yet another state.

Each time the governor appoints an investigative panel, which blames everything on overcrowding, poor facilities, or mismanagement. The corrections commissioner is then fired, and the cycle begins again.

But during a visit to a western penitentiary, site of two recent riots, I discovered what I believe is the real root of this rash of violence.

The prison is a cluster of handsome brick buildings surrounded by gentle hills. But for the fences it might be mistaken for a college campus.

Inside the steel gates, however, it was prison—and it was tense. The corrections commissioner and the warden both looked harried, even as they assured me everything was under control.

Most prisoners wouldn't talk much, but they spoke volumes with their darting glances. Where the riots had broken out, a thick cement wall was but a pile of rubble—frenzied inmates had punched it out with their bare fists! One wing was charred ruins, with toilets ripped out of the walls and debris everywhere. Angry prisoners told me that the place would soon erupt again.

There were no obvious reasons. Atypically, the prison was not overcrowded; the facilities were excellent and the staff well-trained.

Yet inmates had beaten out a cement wall with their bare fists. Why?

The warden had no explanation. "But," he said, "of course we have no work here—only 100 jobs for 800 men. We make work."

"*Make work*." On the flight back to Washington I couldn't forget those words—nor the devastated cellblock. In his offhand remark, the warden may very well have provided the key to the unrest.

The nation is indebted to Chief Justice Burger, who has crusaded for more inmate jobs, recently advocating the establishment of prison factories. I've discussed these proposals with the Chief Justice and firmly believe he's on the right track.

Those who argue for prison jobs usually do so on the grounds that they are important for rehabilitation: Offenders need vocational skills when they get out.

That's true enough. But I think there's a more crucial theological reason as well, one that explains why our prisons drive men to the despair I saw in that western institution.

In the created world around us we can readily see order, harmony, and purpose; this is powerful evidence for the existence of a personal, orderly, and purposeful Creator.

This argument, which theologians call the teleological case for the existence of God, leads inescapably to a further conclusion: Like the universe, man is created by God—in His very image. Thus, man is imbued with the same sense of purpose evident in his Creator. This affects not only our overall perception of life, but practical, everyday relationships, recreation, and *work*.

That man cannot live without purpose was captured by the great Russian novelist Fyodor Dostoyevski, imprisoned for ten years during a period of czarist repression.

Dostoyevski wrote, "If one wanted to crush, to annihilate a

man utterly, to inflict on him the most terrible of punishments . . .
one need only give him work of an absolutely, completely useless
and irrational character." In useful hard labor, he continued, "there
is a sense and meaning. . . . But if he [the inmate] had to . . . pound
sand, to move a heap of earth from one place to another and back
again—I believe the convict would hang himself . . . preferring
rather to die than to endure such humiliation, shame and torture."

Some of Hitler's henchmen must have read Dostoyevski.
Eugene Heimler, a Holocaust survivor, wrote of an experiment in
which Jews who had been working in a prison factory were suddenly ordered to move sand from one end of their camp to
another—back and forth, over a period of weeks.

Many prisoners who had been able to cling to life even while
working for their hated captors now went berserk and were shot by
guards. Others threw themselves into the electrified wire fence, caus-
ing the commandant to remark one day that "now there is no need
to use the crematoria."

This is why it is so crucial to expose the widespread illusion
about punishment and prisons in America today. Some on the liberal side believe we can make modern and humane facilities which
will "cure" criminals of their errant behavior; many on the conservative side confuse prison and punishment by arguing we should
simply lock everyone up and "teach them a lesson."

The result is a national policy which stuffs our facilities with
humanity, half of them nonviolent, gives them nothing meaningful
to do, then stands back in amazement when prisoners riot.

Punishment? Yes. Biblical justice demands it. And prisons are
necessary to separate dangerous offenders from society. But
confining nondangerous men and women with nothing to do, driving them to the brink of their sanity?

No. In doing so we can expect not only prison riots, but the
wrath of a personal Creator who demands purpose and dignity for
those He creates in His image.

September 1985

Chapter Forty-eight

Of Mice and Men—
Prisons and Punishment: III

A few years ago a modest research psychologist undertook the not-so-modest project of creating utopia on earth.

Dr. John Calhoon of the National Institute of Mental Health constructed sixteen-room apartment units in which residents would have regular meals, social opportunities, and a complete security system.

The 160 occupants were, of course, mice. But Calhoon believed his experiment would provide valuable insights into human behavior. If so, what happened in "paradise" raises startling questions about life on this shrinking planet.

The mice settled into the good life—eat, drink and be merry. Being merry, they were also prolific: 400 mice in the first litter.

But the young mice were quickly crowded out. They huddled together, motionless but for occasional outbursts of violence. As they became more congested, many withdrew to simply eat, drink, and sleep. Reproduction ceased. Most frightening of all, their passive-aggressive behavior seemed irreversible. The damage could not be remedied, Calhoon believed, even if a resident were transferred into a normal mouse habitat.

And after five years of abundant food and water, protected from predators, disease, and mousetraps, the entire mouse community had died. Simply crowded to death.

While the Calhoon experiments were intended to warn of the dangers of crowded ghettos, I believe they provide an even more apt parable for America's prisons.

The prison population is increasing fifteen times faster than the general population; today 464,000 men and women are serving time, two-thirds in states under court orders to relieve overcrowding. $7.4 billion is being spent for new construction, but as new prisons open, they are jammed beyond capacity almost overnight.

Tragically, there is no relief in sight. The inmate population is expected to rise by 35 percent in the next five years. Average price tags of $80,000 per maximum security cell (not to mention the $17,000 per year to maintain a prisoner, which does not include construction financing, lost taxes, and welfare payments to inmates' families) could bankrupt many states.

But these shocking statistics fail to capture the depth of human devastation. San Quentin inmates have less space than California law requires for dogs in licensed kennels. In Chicago's Cook County Jail, tuberculosis infected 71 percent of the inmates packed in one cell-block. Across the nation, most of the bloody riots of the last fifteen years have been attributed directly to overcrowded conditions.

I see the effects of overcrowding firsthand in almost every prison I visit. In the most notorious cellblock of an ancient Midwestern prison there were double bunks in each six-by-nine-foot cell. Some nights a third inmate was made to sleep under the bottom bunk on the grimy concrete floor. Like Dr. Calhoon's mice, the long-timers seemed withdrawn, sullen, passive.

Then we came to a cell with only one bunk. A grinning, younger inmate thrust his hand through the bars to shake mine.

"How come you're here by yourself?" I asked.

Still grinning, he replied without hesitation, "Because I'd kill anybody they'd put in here."

The prison authorities believed him; so did I.

And the evidence is, as Dr. Calhoon suggested, that such damage from overcrowding is permanent. According to the FBI, 74 percent of those released from prison are rearrested within four years. On the outside, prisoners who are violent and aggressive continue that behavior; those who have withdrawn are just as helpless.

What is being done? Some states are blindly spending billions for new prisons. That's good news for the architects and builders who are generous contributors to the campaigns of local politicians. But it's bad news for the public.

The truth is, new prison construction can never catch up. California's corrections commissioner announced recently that when the $1.2 billion worth of new prisons is completed, there will still be a 10,000-cell shortage. Prisons are like parking lots—once built, they get filled up.

Fortunately, other states are considering alternatives for non-violent offenders—who make up 50 percent of the prison population.

Florida, for example, where Prison Fellowship worked with lawmakers who faced facts and adopted model legislation two years ago utilizing restitution, expanded probation, and early release programs. The prison population has stabilized, wholesale construction has been averted, overcrowding eased—and the crime rate declined 6.9 percent.

We need such courageous action from lawmakers in every state. For to ignore the current crisis would be tantamount to repeating Dr. Calhoon's experiment on a national scale—not with mice, but with a half-million humans.

October 1985

Chapter Forty-nine

Reading, Writing, and Crime

B e glad you can read this page. If you couldn't and you happened to get into trouble, you might find yourself in prison for a long while.

This may sound absurd, but it is the result of an announcement made by the governor of an eastern state. Anxious to curb crime, he referred to extra funds earmarked for prison education as a "no read, no release" parole policy during a press conference.

On the surface his reasoning seems sensible: if people can't read, they are less employable, so more likely to commit crimes. Teaching illiterate inmates to read should thus reduce recidivism.

No one faults the governor's goal, but his proposal stirred a national ruckus. The ACLU, which still clings to the humanistic notion that education will stop crime, at first applauded, then abruptly about-faced when the press pointed out that the proposal was tantamount to imprisoning people for illiteracy.

Others, including Prison Fellowship, protested that parole should be earned by good behavior and determined by public safety, not reading speed. Although literacy programs are worthwhile tools to equip inmates with needed skills, they do not ensure a drop in crime.

The real problem with the governor's words is that they perpetuate a now-thoroughly discredited myth about the cause of crime that dates back to the thirties and forties. It was fashionable then to view crime as a social sickness: "Good" people went bad because they lived in ghettos or were deprived or discriminated against.

Thus, criminals were not responsible for their actions. They were victims, and society was to blame. The proper response, therefore, was to clean up societal ills that caused crime and "treat" the criminal like any other sick person.

This gave birth to the liberal idea that offenders should not be punished but rehabilitated. It all sounded very humanitarian; so, to accommodate all those who needed to be healed of criminal behavior, we built more and more prisons—and jammed them full.

There was only one problem with this therapeutic approach. It didn't work. Its legacy is the highest crime rate in the world and the third-largest prison population per capita. (The United States falls behind only the Soviet Union and South Africa.)

In light of this failure, the reasonable person must rethink both the cause of crime and the purpose of prison. A central tenet of Judeo-Christian belief is that individuals are morally responsible for their actions. Deprivations can be factors in crime, but wrong moral choices—what the Bible calls sin—are the heart of the problem. Prisons can't rehabilitate because they can't "cure" sin. So imprisonment should be used, not as therapy, but to punish and confine dangerous offenders.

Secular scholars have been coming to this view as well. I've mentioned the landmark study of psychologists Samenow and Yochelson, *The Criminal Personality*, which concluded that crime is a moral problem. The answer, as they put it, is "conversion" of the individual.

Another recent important contribution in this area is *Crime and Human Nature*, by Harvard professors James Wilson and Richard Herrenstein. Though they argue that factors such as intellect and genetic characteristics may influence behavior, they conclude that crime is a function of individual choice. These choices are determined by one's moral conscience—which is shaped early in life and most crucially by the family.

If the key to stopping crime is early moral training, as Wilson and Herrenstein conclude, then we are in big trouble. As a recent CBS TV documentary on the vanishing family in the inner city made all too clear, the same social engineering policies of forty years ago that gave us overcrowded, ineffective prisons have also cultivated a patronizing welfare system in our ghettos, making it economically advantageous to have children out of wedlock.

Thus, correspondent Bill Moyers pointed out, more than half of today's inner-city babies are born to unmarried, teenage mothers. Tragically, the majority of children in crime-prone areas are growing up with little, if any, family moral guidance.

They then enter schools which have been studiously sterilized of moral influence by so-called value clarification. To cite one example, the *New York Times* recently reported on a New Jersey high-school class in which students were asked their opinions on the conduct of a young woman who found $1,000 and turned it in. All fifteen said she was a fool.

A reporter asked why the students' guidance counselor didn't offer his opinion. He explained, "If I come from the position of what is right and what is wrong, then I'm not their counselor."

I realize we live in an upside-down world, but I find it ironic: governors announcing million-dollar proposals to teach convicts to read, while schools can't teach right and wrong.

Certainly we must do something about crime. But let's be realistic. Literacy doesn't shape character. Teaching convicts to read—worthy though that may be—will not really help stop crime. What will help is teaching youngsters moral values in our homes and schools, so they won't end up in prison in the first place.

May 1986

Chapter Fifty

Real Christianity

These have not been the best of times for Christian ministers and ministries. Disclosures of sexual indiscretions, air-conditioned dog houses, and gold-plated bathroom fixtures have given the press a field day.

The television coverage has resembled an extended episode of "Dynasty," focusing on Christian celebrities bedecked in expensive jewelry leaving palatial estates in Mercedes limousines.

The result of the extraordinary press attention has been to stereotype all Christians as flamboyant frauds. An old friend jokingly told me that he could finally understand my conversion: "Big money," he said. "Better than practicing law!" This reaction is understandable, particularly when some Christian leaders gleefully babble that "economic prosperity is God's way of rewarding those who are faithful to Him."

Admittedly, there are "operators" in every profession—but the current caricature of Christian leaders is unfair and untrue. Over the past twelve years I've come to know thousands of ministers, the vast majority of whom are serving at great sacrifice. I've met pastors who care far more about church discipline than church growth, missionaries who live under conditions I could not, and brilliant men and women working at Christian institutions for half the salary they might enjoy in the secular world.

I thought about all this a few weeks ago [1987] as I waited my turn to speak at a Nashville meeting honoring one of our field staff, Bob McGuire.

Bob joined Prison Fellowship as our Tennessee area director in 1983. He immediately began crisscrossing Tennessee, organizing volunteer groups across the state. Five months later his eyesight, weakened from an eighteen-year battle with diabetes, began to deteriorate. But he refused to cut back on his schedule—until the day he drove the wrong way down a one-way street. Laser surgery was unsuccessful; soon Bob was legally blind.

Bob might well have decided to retire on disability compensation and take life easy. But he believed that God had called him, and he decided to stay in ministry, even though blind, even though it was hard.

He had once described himself as a "macho type"; now he struggled to accept forced dependence upon others. He reasoned, "If I had felt that God would work only through my strengths or my physical abilities, what would I have left? Nothing. But God has shown me that He doesn't work through all that. And my strength is not in my abilities, but in my faith in God. It's His strength through my weakness that appears to people." Bob's wife, Jo-Ann, became more than his partner in ministry. She became his eyes, driving him all over the state and walking him by the hand through prison cellblocks.

That dependence gave the McGuires a great opportunity to witness for Christ. The inmates saw that a man in a prison of his own had come to release them from their bonds. Miracles came out of Bob's infirmity. As Jo-Ann put it, "As Bob grew physically weaker, we saw greater moves of God through him."

A clear example of that came during a Memphis in-prison seminar. Because each of the fifty inmates attending had his own view on the discussion topic (Biblical authority) the seminar had dissolved into an angry gripe session. The instructor was at a loss as to how he could make the point that humility before God is the key to achieving true authority. Then Bob and Jo-Ann mutually had an inspiration.

At their suggestion, the chaplain filled a basin with water and placed it and a stack of towels at the front of the room. With tears welling in his eyes, Bob addressed the inmates. He had once been supremely self-reliant, he said, but through his blindness he had learned the humility of being served by others. And that's precisely what the leaders would teach the inmates.

One by one the prisoners came forward. Their arrogance dissolved as seminar leaders washed their feet. Ten men received Christ; seventeen others rededicated their lives to Him. In voices often broken by sobs, they testified that they would model their lives after what they had seen so vividly in the McGuires—the spirit of true servanthood.

Every time I read an article about a so-called Christian leader living in splendor, I think of Bob McGuire, who left his modest Georgia home to live in a small Nashville apartment so he could serve prisoners. And when I see glossy photos of Christian celebrities riding in long, black limousines, I think of Bob and Jo-Ann driving their old Volvo—with more than 100,000 miles on it—all over Tennessee. And whenever I see pictures of Christian leaders surrounded by admiring worshipers, I envision Bob McGuire orchestrating a foot-washing session in a dismal Tennessee prison. When I read of people getting rich on ministry, I think of Bob McGuire, who never made more than $25,000 a year in his life and shared whatever he had with others.

I only wish the national press, so derisive toward Christians, could interview Bob. But they won't have that opportunity: Bob recently lost his long battle with diabetes and left us to join the Savior he had served so faithfully.

And that's why I was at that meeting in Nashville. It was a memorial service for Bob McGuire. Volunteers, chaplains, and ex-prisoners came from all over the state to pay their respects to one who had served "the least of these" so selflessly. And all of us in that crowded church could hear the echo of our Lord's commendation to our brother: "Well done, good and faithful servant."

As a result of today's media stereotypes, the public may see Christian ministers as power-hungry money-grubbers. But the truth of the matter is to be found in the lives of men and women like Bob McGuire—hundreds of thousands around the world who sacrificially live out the gospel in humble service to others.

And that's real Christianity.

September 1987

Chapter Fifty-one

Lessons from the East

It's enough to boggle your mind.

Four billion dollars' worth of new prisons now under construction. The President trying to keep his campaign promise to double federal prison capacity in four years: three billion more dollars. A projected cost of fifty billion dollars if the government were to build all the prison spaces needed to meet *current* demand. That's nearly $1,000 in taxes per typical U.S. family.

Even those billions would be money well spent if they eased crime's choke hold on our nation. But crime rates are rising. So are recidivism rates. The most advanced nation on earth is held hostage by fear of crime and the huge costs of trying to crush it.

But I recently discovered a glimmer of hope—in a rather unlikely place.

Sometimes when I describe my visits to Third-World prisons, people shrink back in horror, visions from movies like *Midnight Express* stalking their minds. But during my trip to the Far East I discovered that "Made in the U.S.A." doesn't always assure the best quality—particularly when it applies to prisons.

In the Philippines I visited Muntinlupa Prison. Two years ago it housed 12,000 inmates and was run by prison gangs. Then General Goyena, a member of the Prison Fellowship Philippines board of directors, was appointed head of the prison system. He cracked down on the gangs, reduced the prison population by putting nonviolent offenders in nonprison punishments, and introduced new work programs.

As I walked through housing units, the prisoners were busily making crafts such as picture frames, wooden boxes, and handsome sculptures. These are sold through a prison industry arrangement; the inmates thus have their own money to put in their commissary accounts. More important, they are able to send money to their families, who would otherwise fall by the wayside.

What struck me most, though, was that in this maximum-security unit, the men were carving with razor-sharp knives. I asked the warden if this created a security risk. "Oh, no," he said. "They realize that if there were any trouble, their knives would be taken away. And their knives are their livelihood."

It was clear that their work gave the inmates a sense of pride and dignity. They enthusiastically showed me the fine details and expertise of their carving. The act of productivity was giving them something that U.S. prisons often rob from inmates.

In the U.S., relatively few prisoners are gainfully employed. The rest are most often idle and apathetic. In Muntinlupa the inmates were alert, smiling, productive. The truth that purposeful work, by its very nature, ennobles was clear in their attitudes.

What I saw in Singapore was even more impressive. I visited Changi prison, notorious since the Japanese held Allied POWs there. Today private industry bids for the opportunity to produce products inside Changi. The prisons actually make money on these prison industries, which are managed by a quasi-governmental corporation.

Organized in assembly lines, the inmates were manufacturing circuit boards and beautiful rosewood furniture.

I've seen little of this in U.S. prisons—except, perhaps, PRIDE, Jack Eckerd's excellent experiment in Florida.

I'm aware of the cultural differences between the Far East and the U.S. The Eastern mind-set is intrinsically more communitarian, with less focus on the individual than in the West. The military-style nature of Asian prisons would not adapt easily in the U.S. And some aspects of cultural and political life in the East are far more repressive than we would tolerate here.

I am not suggesting that prison industries, on their own, can rehabilitate. But our nation can learn something about the positive nature of work for prisoners. As Christians we should be particularly aware of this: We believe that man was created in God's image and is therefore a purposeful creation. As Carl Henry has said, "Locking up a person to idleness would be a contradiction of his essential dignity because man, by creation, was a creature made for work rather than for idleness."

We've seen this in our Community Service Projects, in which inmates are furloughed to repair the homes of needy people. Prisoners gain a sense of self-esteem; the community gains needed work done for free. As one inmate said, "I figure I can either lie on my prison bunk and cost taxpayers about $16,000 a year, or I can be out here doing something productive, paying society back."

That same principle could well be applied inside prison walls. The benefits—to morale, to prison budgets, to inmates' families—make it well worthwhile.

American prisons are costing us billions. Why not use a few thousand of that for plane tickets to Muntinlupa and Changi prisons for the President, attorney general, and a few other well-placed leaders. What they would see there, in terms of the productive nature of work and its reinforcement of human dignity, could not help but provide ideas to address the prison crisis in our own nation.

Now, *that* would be money well spent.

February 1989

Chapter Fifty-two

Reflecting the Incarnation

"Have this attitude in yourselves which was also in Christ Jesus, who, although He existed in the form of God, did not regard equality with God a thing to be grasped, but emptied Himself, taking the form of a bondservant . . ." (Philippians 2:5-7, NASB).

This Christmas [1987] I and hundreds of Prison Fellowship volunteers will go into prison to celebrate the birth of Christ. Non-Christian friends often assume we do so out of pity or sentimentality. "Oh, isn't that nice," they respond. "Now *there's* the real meaning of Christmas." It's as if lonely prisoners are in the same category as poor Tiny Tim Cratchit, and we who visit them are Yuletide humanitarians.

Of course we go to comfort inmates. But there is a deeper motivation, one that has to do with the reason we celebrate Christmas at all. For in those cold, dank prisons, I have discovered, one experiences the mystery of the Incarnation in a profound way. One of the most poignant illustrations of this comes from strife-torn Northern Ireland.

Northern Ireland has been divided for centuries by conflicts between Protestants and Catholics. The issues are not only religious, however, but economic, cultural, and political. Bullets have all too often replaced ballots; assassinations and terrorism are rampant. Every proposed political solution has been frustrated.

One of the bleakest chapters in Northern Ireland's prison history took place from roughly 1979 to 1981, when terrorist inmates of Belfast's Maze Prison embarked upon a series of prison strikes to frustrate the British government and gain world publicity for their cause.

Prisoners on one such strike, the dirty protest, refused to wash, refused to wear clothing, refused to leave their cells. Covered only by a blanket with a ragged hole cut out for the head, they sat on the concrete floor. They smeared their excrement on the walls and rinsed their hands with their urine. Their hair and beards grew long and knotted, streaked with filth.

Though the prisoners grew accustomed to the incredible stench, officers often vomited and fainted. Visitors were nonexistent.

That is, except for Gladys Blackburne.

On Christmas Eve 1980, Gladys Blackburne was having tea in her small Belfast flat. A retired schoolteacher in her mid-sixties, Miss Blackburne was an inch shy of five feet. With gently curled gray hair, pearls, and sensible shoes, she had a determined way about her.

Miss Blackburne had long taken Northern Ireland's civil unrest personally, asking God to show her what she could do to honor Him in a land where "the name of Jesus was being dragged in the gutter." And she had been doing what she believed God had required of her: to be the best citizen she could in her small, troubled nation, and to show the love of Christ to those in need.

Miss Blackburne had gotten herself on the Maze Prison Board of Visitors and consequently had access to any part of the prison, day or night.

So on this Christmas Eve, 1980, Miss Blackburne drank her tea and prayed about how God would have her celebrate the birth of His Son. *I must do something as near as possible to what Jesus*

*did when He left His home in glory and was born in a Bethlehem
stable*, she thought.

A stable, she repeated to herself. *Does God want me to go to
the Maze—into the dirty protest, where the cells smell like stables?
I can't do that.*

But Gladys Blackburne was not a person to take God's direction lightly. As she put on her coat and gloves, she prayed for the
grace to handle what she would find at the Maze.

She hitched a ride to the prison and cleared the laborious security checks. Before she got to the dirty protesters, however, a
Christian prison officer took her aside. "There's a lad in a different
wing who's asking a lot of questions about Christianity," he said.
"Why don't you visit him first?"

Thus it was that Gladys Blackburne spent her Christmas Eve,
as she would the next several years, in the Maze Prison among the
inmates. And thus it was that she met Chips, a young inmate who
had studied terrorism, Marxism, fascism, and atheism, finding no
answers. Gladys Blackburne, sitting there on a prison chair, her feet
barely touching the floor, told Chips about Jesus Christ—born
nearly 2,000 years earlier to heal the hearts of those who were broken. And later that Christmas Eve, while Gladys Blackburne went
on to sit with the dirty protesters and lead them in Christmas carols,
Chips committed his life to Jesus Christ.

Today Chips is a free man, a Prison Fellowship volunteer, and
a student at a Christian college. He is part of a vibrant fellowship
of ex-prisoners, both Catholic and Protestant, who are bound
together as brothers ready to lay down their lives for one
another—powerful witnesses of God's reconciling love in that frac-
tured place called Belfast. And Gladys Blackburne is still visiting
those in need.

The world may look at people like her and smile benignly
about the "spirit of Christmas." But Miss Blackburne and the thousands of Prison Fellowship volunteers around the world are not
mere do-gooders. Rather, out of Biblical obedience they go into the
miserable holes called prisons to pour themselves out for those in

need; they are thus reflecting the Incarnation of the God who came to a miserable earth to pour Himself out for us.

Of course, not all of us can go into prison. But at Christmas may we examine our hearts and be bold enough, each in his or her own way, to replicate Christ's great sacrifice for us—and thus experience the glorious mystery of the Incarnation.

December 1987

Index